3 Steps to Instant Profits!

By **T.J. Rohleder**
(a.k.a. "The Blue Jeans Millionaire")

Other Great Titles from T.J. Rohleder:

Ruthless Marketing Secrets (Series)
The 2-Step Marketing Secret That Never Fails
Stealth Marketing
The Power of Hype
Money Machine
Instant Cash Flow
The Blue Jeans Millionaire
How to Turn Your Kitchen or Spare Bedroom into a Cash Machine
The Black Book of Marketing Secrets (Series)
The Ultimate Wealth-Maker
Four Magical Secrets to Building a Fabulous Fortune
The Ruthless Marketing Attack
How to Get Super Rich in the Opportunity Market
$60,000.00 in 90 Days
How to Start Your Own Million Dollar Business
Fast Track to Riches
Five Secrets That Will Triple Your Profits
Ruthless Copywriting Strategies
25 Direct Mail Success Secrets That Can Make You Rich
Ruthless Marketing
24 Simple and Easy Ways to Get Rich Quick
How to Create a Hot Selling Internet Product in One Day
50 in 50
Secrets of the Blue Jeans Millionaire
Shortcut Secrets to Creating High-Profit Products
Foolproof Secrets of Sucessful Millionaires
How to Make Millions While Sitting on Your Ass
500 Ways to Get More People to Give You More Money

FIRST EDITION

ISBN 1-933356-84-7

TABLE OF CONTENTS

Introduction:

By T.J. Rohleder

THANK YOU for purchasing this book and taking the time to carefully go over it. As you'll see, this can give you A MAJOR ADVANTAGE over almost ALL of your competitors!

IT'S TRUE! Most of your competitors are TERRIBLE MARKETERS. These people suffer from the delusion of thinking that all they have to do to succeed in the market is to deliver THE HIGHEST QUALITY PRODUCT OR SERVICE. Unfortunately, many of these people are STRUGGLING FINANCIALLY and going out of business. You see, **in today's overcrowded and over-competitive marketplace, it's NEVER the companies who deliver the best products or services who make it—it's the ones who do the best marketing.** And the more you understand about marketing, the more you'll realize that VERY FEW of your competitors truly understand even the BASIC RULES of what good marketing is all about.

But YOU won't make this mistake! By going over this book [and taking advantage of my 'FREE GIFT OFFER' that I'll tell you about in a minute!]—you will know <u>EXACTLY</u> what you must do to find, get, and keep MORE of the very best customers and clients in your marketplace. And because of that fact, you will have A VERY REAL ADVANTAGE over all of your competitors that will enable you to DOMINATE your market and get all the money that could and should be yours!

3 STEPS TO INSTANT PROFITS!

So when I tell you that "Your decision to purchase this book and take the time to go over it is one of the wisest things you can do"—I MEAN IT!

Good marketing is YOUR SECRET POWER to find, get, and keep MORE of the very best customers and clients in your marketplace. **There are ONLY SO MANY of these great clients and customers and the MORE you understand about marketing, the MORE POWER you'll have to attract them to YOU, instead of your competition.**

One of my early marketing mentors told me that "Marketing takes a day to learn and a lifetime to master." He was right! And, yet, just having A FIRM UNDERSTANDING of the information in CHAPTER ONE of this book will put you light years ahead of almost all of the individuals and companies that are trying to attract the same customers and clients that you need to build your business. And as complicated as all of this can be, it's still VERY SIMPLE. Remember that. Good marketing is simply all the things that you do to ATTRACT and RETAIN the very best prospects in your market. That's it. It's that simple. The problem is: IT CAN BE VERY DIFFICULT to do this!

Today's marketplace is over-crowded and the average prospect has built a very real IMMUNITY to most advertising and marketing messages. Because of this, it TAKES EVEN MORE KNOWLEDGE, SKILL, AND ABILITY to attract and retain these people. BUT DON'T LET THAT DISCOURAGE YOU! The fact that this can be very difficult is the main thing that will always keep your competitors from devoting the time and work that is necessary to become great marketers. Remember that and TAKE PRIVATE PLEASURE in the fact that by purchasing this book [and then taking advantage of my

6

'FREE OFFER' and using it!] you will have A VERY REAL ADVANTAGE over all of the people you compete with.

The bottom line: the better marketer you become, the MORE POWER you will have to find, get, and keep the LARGEST NUMBER of the very best customers and clients in your marketplace. And THAT gives you the power to TOTALLY DOMINATE your market!

Of course, maybe you don't want to 'DOMINATE YOUR MARKET' and instead, you just want to build a SUPER PROFITABLE BUSINESS... IF SO, this book [and my FREE GIFT that's waiting for you on the Internet!] will let you do this!

So please TAKE THE TIME to carefully go over this book. Start with Chapter One, which is the theme behind the TITLE OF THIS BOOK and discover the ONLY 3 WAYS that you can build your business. Then go on to the other chapters and discover even more PROVEN MARKETING SECRETS that can give you the power to find, get, and keep MORE of the very best customers and clients.

And to reward you for purchasing this book, I have...

A great FREE business-building gift for you!

Yes, I have a gift waiting for you that can DRAMATICALLY INCREASE YOUR SALES AND PROFITS! Here's what it's all about: I spent TEN FULL YEARS writing down all of the greatest marketing and success secrets I discovered during that time period. Each day I took a few notes and, at the end of a decade, I had a GIANT LIST of 6,159 powerful secrets! This list is ALMOST 1,000 PAGES of hardcore money-making ideas and strategies!** **Best of all, this massive collection is now YOURS ABSOLUTELY FREE!** Just go to: www.6159FreeSecrets.com and get it NOW! As you'll see, this complete collection of 6,159 of my greatest marketing and success secrets, far more valuable than those you can buy from others for $495 to $997, is absolutely **FREE.** No cost, no obligation.

Why am I giving away this GIANT COLLECTION of secrets, that took ONE DECADE to discover and compile, FOR FREE? That's simple: I believe many of the people who receive these 6,159 secrets in this huge 955 page PDF document will want to obtain some of our other books and audio programs and participate in our special COACHING PROGRAMS. However, you are NOT obligated to buy anything—now or ever.

I know you're serious about making more money or you wouldn't be reading this. So go to: www.6159FreeSecrets.com and get this complete collection of 6,159 of my greatest marketing and success secrets right now! **You'll get this GREAT FREE GIFT in the next few minutes, just for letting me add you to my Client mailing list,** and I'll stay in CLOSE TOUCH with you... and do all I can to help you make even more money with my proven marketing strategies and methods.

So with all this said, let's begin...

** WARNING: This complete collection of 6,159 marketing and success secrets contains MANY CONTROVERSIAL ideas and methods. Also, it was originally written for MY EYES ONLY and for a few VERY CLOSE FRIENDS. Therefore, the language is X-RATED in some places [I got VERY EXCITED when I wrote many of these ideas and used VERY FOUL LANGUAGE to get my ideas across!] so 'IF' you are EASILY OFFENDED or do NOT want to read anything OFFENSIVE, then please do both of us a favor and DO NOT go to my website and download this FREE gift. THANK YOU for your understanding.

CHAPTER ONE

There are only 3 ways to build a business:

1. Get more customers.

2. Sell more high-ticket items — for bigger profits.

3. Sell more often to your customers!

Almost all million-dollar marketing ideas are transferable from one business to another.

The Basics of Building a Business

It's all about the basics. Always.

There are so many different kinds of businesses, and everybody thinks that theirs is unique. At some level they're absolutely correct: their business *is* unique, no question about it. But there are common denominators to every business in the world, and I think it's really important to focus on those, especially during the planning stages. **Whenever you get confused, whenever you get frustrated, go back to the basics.** Take a deep breath, calm yourself down, and think about that.

I'll be revealing a number of basic formulas, and the following is one of the *most* basic. I like to go back to it again and again, whenever I get confused about all the possible choices. It goes like this: **There are only *three ways* to build a business.** With rare exceptions, this applies to every business there is. **The first way to build your business is to get more customers. The second way to build a business is to sell more big-ticket items for greater profits per transaction. The third way is to sell more often to your existing customers.**

Those are pretty straightforward... but people tend to screw themselves out of money regularly by not keeping those three simple options in mind. Don't shoot yourself in the foot this way. Start paying attention to how other companies are using all these ways to make money. **Get good at getting on the other**

side of the cash register, as we like to say, and realize that all the ideas that these other people are using to get more customers, or get them to come back more often, or get them to spend more money, are all potentially transferable from their business to yours.

Whenever you start thinking, "Oh, my business is different, you don't understand," then you're not being very open and receptive to new ideas. **And you've *got* be open and receptive.** There's a time for shooting down ideas, or for editing them and trying to pick them apart and trying to see which ones are better than others... but it's not in the very beginning. Stay open. Stay receptive. **Look for ways that other companies are doing these three things I've mentioned.**

Now, everybody realizes that you have to keep trying to attract new customers. In fact, that's what most business owners spend most of their time on. And that's great, **but the other two ways are how you make all your real profits, and you ignore them at your peril.** What usually ends up happening is that these folks aren't doing anything special for their old customers. **Therefore, you've got to have a marketing system in place to acquire new customers automatically while you take care of your older customers directly.** You build your marketing system once and set it in place; afterward, it just keeps working for you, with some minor modifications along the way. You can't just set it and forget it; you've got to continue to work on it, make tweaks, change it, and adjust it.

For over two decades now, we've done new customer acquisition on a weekly basis. That's part of our marketing system. Every week, we send out tens of thousands of direct mail packages. Come rain or shine, 52 weeks a year, we've got something out there to attract new customers. That's how we build our business the first way. **The second way is by selling high ticket items.** For example, we've just put together a new coaching program that comes in two varieties. The first sells for just under $5,000. The second costs just under $10,000. Just one $5,000 or $10,000 sale can make a big difference—can pay some bills—and that's important very, very important.

The third way to build your business is to sell to your customers more often. You have to keep re-inviting people to do business with you. Stay in touch with them; you almost can't do so often enough. A lot of people are afraid of that possibility, which never ceases to amaze me. They're so afraid that they're going to alienate their customers by trying to sell too often, and yet very few ever even come close to doing that. Let me tell you this: **if you're not making offers constantly, your customers are out there buying from your competitors.** If you think your customers are loyal to you and only you, you're crazy! In most markets, they're buying from other people too—not just your direct competitors, but indirect competitors as well.

Look: they've got money, so you've got to keep making them offers to try to resell them again and again, even if your business isn't one where there are a lot of big-ticket items. That's the case with our new pet boutique, but we're doing things within that business. We're planning to hold special events on a regular basis—events that can potentially make us thousands of dollars in a weekend, which is a pretty good haul for a little retail store. So we're always asking ourselves: Where's the big payday? Where's the event that's going to bring in the money all at once? How can we pull that off?

You should always be thinking about this. These are the *only* three ways to build a business. **Anytime you're frustrated or confused, go back to the basics.** You've got to have strategies in place for getting more customers, strategies for selling to those customers more often, and strategies for selling big ticket items (or hosting profitable events). This is simplicity itself. It's not one of those complex formulas some business gurus push. You don't have to run this formula by the Board, or get buy-in from dozens of people. There really are only three ways to build your business; and if your business is struggling, you need to implement systems to strengthen each point. When you listen to people advise you on how to fix your business, unless they're talking about these three things in some way or another, they're barking up the wrong tree. **Get more people to visit your store, or get more people to respond to your direct mail offers. Get them to spend more money on you. Get them to buy from you repeatedly. It's not rocket science.**

So how do you do all that? I recommend that you use some form of DRM you can track. It's one thing to hear local business people say, "I'm doing all kinds of things to bring people into my store. I've got word of mouth; I've got my Yellow Page ad, and yeah, I've got some ads running in the Valpak. I've even got a TV commercial and a radio spot. I support some local baseball and basketball teams, too, so my name's on the backs of their jerseys." So they've got all these things going on, which is great—but they have no way of knowing where their customer is coming from.

What you need to do is more of what you know worked

in the past... but unless you can track where your customers are coming from, you don't really *know* what's working. So you're stuck going, "OK, I have this all-or-nothing approach. I've got to continue doing more things to bring people in to my business, but I don't know what stuff's working." By using trackable DRM methods, you can fix that problem. **You can know where your customers are coming from most of the time, and you can make more decisions to advertise in just those ways.** If you find out that these few magazines are bringing you your best response, continue running ads in those magazines. If you find that your Yellow Page ad isn't working at all, well, you certainly don't need to continue running a full page ad, do you? Maybe you can get by with a smaller one, or maybe you can change that ad to offer a coupon or some direct response mechanism that gets people to acknowledge they responded specifically to that offer. Those are effective, trackable ways to get more customers to come into your store the first time.

When it comes to selling more big-ticket items for bigger profits, you might have to get a little creative, depending on the marketplace you're in and the product or services you sell. Maybe you don't have a high-dollar item, but you probably do. If you've got a retail store and your average item only sells for $5-10, you probably have a few things that sell for $20-50; you just don't have that many of them. **Even if you're not selling expensive items, you can try to do things to put emphasis on your *more* expensive items.** What kinds of promotions can you run to get people to always want to buy, or at least *consider* buying, those items? Can you bundle them in a package? Can you run a special offer so people are at least more inclined to pay attention to the fact that you have those expensive items available? Maybe people don't even see them because they're buried in the back of your store. Maybe you can bring those items up closer to the cash register. Or maybe you can increase your average ticket. If the average person comes into your store and spends $20, maybe you can get that average up closer to $30 or $40. Maybe you can offer some add-ons while they're at the cash register. "While you're at the store, did you know we have these on sale here? You can take any two of these for $10."

Lastly: sell more often to your customers. Are you doing any database marketing right now? If not, you can probably increase the amount of times your customers do business with you just by repeatedly reminding them to come back to your store. Maybe your average customer only shops with you once a year, because that's about how often they think about you. **Well, just by reminding them to come back into your store on a more regular basis, you'll get more of them to do just that.**

Maybe you have a newsletter that you send out by email, or even snail mail. Maybe it's full of stories from some of your favorite customers. You have different things that are of interest to your target marketplace, and each time you include a coupon or a special offer that's good until the end of that month. They can come into the store and get this particular product for this price, or they can pick any of *these* items and get 10% off. **Consider some kind of continuity program; that's another way to instantly increase the amount of your customers coming back.** Give them an automated way to do business with you. Maybe you've got a product that could be sold on a month-to-month basis. Let's say you've got a health business, and it's a supplement they buy. Well, they're probably coming in every once in a while and buying... but maybe you can get them to commit to subscribing to it on a monthly basis, so they don't even have to come into the store. Or maybe they *do* have to come into the store to pick it up, because you want them to buy some other stuff while they're there. In any case, you automatically charge their credit card. They're going to commit to buying it every month, and you're going to give them a special price, for example.

Those are the three things to build a business. It's really no more complicated than that, although a lot of people try to *make* it more complicated. **You can increase your business, and build it bigger and better and faster and stronger, just by finding ways to get more customers and by selling more big-ticket items for higher profits more often to the customers you already have.** It's as simple as that. Keep finding ways to make more money. It's out there for you right now, in peoples' credit cards and bank accounts. **You've just got to figure out how to get it, and that's what we're here to help you do.**

CHAPTER TWO

The **names** and **addresses**
of your best customers and their
past buying information can be
worth it's weight in diamonds!

*If you know what to do
with this list!*

Your Customer List is Worth its Weight in Diamonds

The names and addresses of your very best customers—and I mean your *very best* customers—and all their past buying information can be worth their weight in diamonds, if you know what to do with that list. Your good customer list is a very valuable thing—and yet it's shocking to me how many small companies don't even keep a list of their customers at all. Oh, they've got the data; they *could* put it together. It's there somewhere, but they don't do anything with it. I think that's a joke... and it's not a very funny one.

Twenty-five years ago, when I first got started in business, I didn't know anything. I made a lot of mistakes, but I got this one right: I had a little book that I carried with me everywhere. I never let it out of my sight. It was always within three to five feet from me, always, and I called it "my Bible." I remember telling my wife, when we were dating, that I had my Bible with me all the time. Well, in this case my Bible was my list of customers, along with all their contact information—and I constantly called them up, trying to resell them stuff. I did everything else wrong in that business, but that's the one thing that I did right.

It's something that you need to think about, too. As I mentioned in the last section, **you need to segment your customer base. Try to prioritize it, separating your best**

customers from all the rest. Then do everything you can to make them many different offers, repeatedly. This sounds like common sense, and yet I promise you that there's nothing common about it, because most businesses don't do this. **Customers go where they're invited, and they stay where they feel some sense of appreciation.** They enjoy the fact that you understand them and you're trying to serve them and help them. But most people don't even keep a customer list!

Why is this? Well, I know for a fact that it's often based mostly on a rather arrogant attitude that goes, "Hey, my customers know where I am. If they want what I have, they know exactly where to get it." Well, let me tell you: that attitude may have worked in a day and age when consumers didn't have so many choices of where to spend their money, but in today's business world, **it's a recipe for failure.** Some of your competitors are extremely aggressive and very smart—so smart they're dangerous. **Your job is to become a dangerous competitor yourself.** *Your* job is to outfox all of your competitors, to think more strategically and be more aggressive with your marketing, to be more proactive and offensive.

Build your database. Segment it. Stay in touch with these people. Keep track of what different customers buy; that's one way you segment your list. Some customers gravitate to certain products and services, and some gravitate to others, so you can segment them by what they bought from you. **The second general way to segment your list is by how much they bought.** The customers who buy the most from you are your very best customers by default. Now again, that makes sense; but you'd be surprised how few people get this.

Once you've segmented your best customers out, you want to make additional offers to those people. Don't just send them some little newsletter or something like that; make them offers. **Try to come up with special deals for them.** Always try to look for new ways to package whatever it is that you sell. **Realize just how much money you have in that mailing list.** There's tons of money there—a vast amount of potential financial energy. These people know you, they like you, and they trust you. **People want to do business with people they know, like and trust, and they want to do business with people that they've had good experiences with in the past.** Rather than try their luck with somebody new, they'd much rather go back to what they know works for them. That's understandable, and it's easy to see; so take advantage of it. **There's so much money that can be and should be yours, *if* you know how to use the list.**

Here's a quick story to illustrate the concept. We started a business within our business maybe five years ago, and during the first eighteen months, it made us a small fortune. We were just raking it in—bringing in huge sums of money every single month on this little side business. But during the last few years, we've watched our little business-within-a-business go downhill. Hindsight being twenty-twenty, **I know now that one of the factors that caused this was that we didn't take care of our list properly.** Sure, the market has changed a little; that and a couple of other small factors played into the decline. But sometimes when business is really good and money's rolling in, it has almost a hypnotic affect on you... and you get the feeling that it's always going to be that way. Even though you know in the back of your mind that it could change, your emotions get caught up in it.

What was causing that business to do so well for the first eighteen months was the fact that we had so many customers at that time that we were taking the cream right off the top. We were taking advantage of the existing stored energy in our list, and there's not as much stored energy left for our business-within-a-business now. Oh, the business is still a going concern, and we're still finding ways to develop it, but we've tapped most of that potential energy, and for now it's gone.

My point is, you can't ignore that potential. People who've done business with you for a long time trust you, like you, and respect you, and they'll buy more from you. **People are insatiable, so they** *want* **to buy more from you—but you've got to be the one to go out there and** *get* **it.** If you do that with your customer list, if you do it repeatedly and get really good at it, it's almost like creating money out of thin air. Any time you need more money, you just throw an offer out there to your existing customers that's similar to the one they've bought before, and *Boom!* There's more money. You have the power to generate it that easily.

I like the synergy between these last two Ways. The way you avoid wasting time and money on deadbeat prospects is by segmenting your list, so that you can pick out the gold nuggets more easily. That flows right into this concept that the names and addresses of your best customers, and their past buying information, are worth their weight in diamonds. **The caveat here is that you really do have to know what to do with the list.** It does no good to collect the contact info and purchase history of your best customers if you're not doing something with that information. The only reason to have a list is to mail to it or to otherwise communicate with it, according to whatever your business model is. There are all kinds of things you can do with a mailing list.

We've found that direct mailing through the postal service to your customers, even if you're just inviting them to go to your website, can have an impact on your profitability. This has been confirmed by other businesses. Even if you're strictly an online business, this often works better than email follow-ups. Oh, you can still make a good profit that way, but you're limiting yourself because of the huge problems with spamming and email clutter. People are so inundated with email messages that often, your important messages don't get through. **A letter in the mail is warm, it's friendly, it's personable; people take the time to open mail that they receive from somebody they know.** So as you look to communicate with your clients, even if you're an online business you should really consider adding direct mail to the mix—real U.S. Postal service mail, in an envelope.

Now, I do think it's critical to separate bad direct marketing from good direct marketing; I talked earlier about not just sending out a little newsletter. There are all kinds of bad examples of direct mail, especially in the local retail business world. We see people sending out cheesy one-page newsletters that look like they've been copied a thousand times, and they're basically just asking you to come into the store or reminding you they're still there. Often it's a newsletter that doesn't really sell anything or offer any direct benefits. You see some people mailing cheesy postcards that look like glorified business cards;

they basically have the name of the store, their location, their hours, and maybe a little map. Yeah, they remind you that you haven't been there in awhile, or maybe they remind you that that business still exists... **but there's no offer there. There's nothing to draw people in, and that's where these businesses go wrong.**

So when you're using your mailing list, you've got to know what to do with it. You've got to create the kinds of offers that people want to respond to. **Nothing should ever go out of your business without a call to action on it.** That's an important first step: **if you're mailing something to your customers,** *always* **include an offer to get them to come back in.** Even if you're just communicating news and information to them, include a coupon or other special offer, like, "This month, all this merchandise is buy one, get one half price." Or, "Right now we're featuring this on sale." Or, "This whole month, we're going to be featuring this particular brand." Do anything you can do to give people a reason to come in.

And of course, you could do everything from a minimal direct response campaign, something like mailing a coupon or a postcard, to full sales letters and offers where you're actually doing the selling by mail. **In all cases, you're trying to get people to take action right then and there.** So there are all kinds of different variations on that theme; but the main thing is, first, to collect the names and addresses of your best customers and then do something with them. **Use that information to build direct mail campaigns that go out to those people on a regular basis to get them to do more and more business with you.**

The other part of this, which I haven't talked about much so far, is the buying information. It's one thing to build a list of people's names and mailing addresses, but what do you do with their buying information? **Well, one of the things you can do is segment your list based on their purchase history.** Let's say you've got three groups of preferred customers: Customer Lists A, B, and C. The A list is people who have spent more than $1,000 with you. The B list is people who spent more than $500, and your C list is people who have spent more than $100.

Your list segmentation may depend on your product, what your profit margins are, and how much you're selling your products for. If you have products selling for as high as $5000 or $10,000, then the cutoff for your A-list might be rather high. So how do you segment in the first place? By using the information from your database. So you've got to have some kind of point-of-sale software, if you're in the retail world, or some kind of mail order management software if you do business by mail or on the Internet. **You've got to have some kind of database system in place to be able to track purchases, so that you *know* who your best customers are.**

It's easy for us. If I were to go to our administrative department right now and say, **"Give me a list of everybody on our entire customer list who has spent $,1000 with us over the last six months,"** within two minutes I'd have a list. Once I had that list, I could drop a piece of mail to those people saying, "Hey! I'm sending this to you because I know that you spent this much money with me over the last several months, and I'd like to make you a special offer."

Or, if I wanted to say to my administrative personnel, **"I**

want everybody who *hasn't* spent this much money in the last year," I could do a mailing tomorrow that said, "Hey! I'm just sending this letter to you because I noticed that you haven't been doing business with us lately, and I'm wondering why. Did we do something to offend you? We'd like you back, so we're making you this special offer."

Having at your fingertips not only the raw data of the names and mailing addresses, but also their purchase history, lets you target your list a lot more effectively. The idea, again, is to try to find the customers who buy the most often and for the most money. **Both of those things can increase your bottom line.** Of course, you want to keep acquiring new customers, too, because that's one of the basic ways of increasing your profits. But when dealing with your existing customers, you either bring them into the store more often or get them to spend more money. When they come into the store, instead of spending only $20, maybe they're spending $50.

How do you do that? **By collecting the names and addresses of your best customers and their buying histories, so you can segment your customers into different groups, so that you can communicate the most effectively to each one of those groups.** That's what having the names and addresses of your best customers can do for you.

CHAPTER THREE

♥ ♥ ♥ ♥ ♥

Selling is like the ritual of dating — the more you need them — the faster they run.

<u>You</u> <u>must</u> <u>let</u> <u>them</u> <u>come</u> <u>to</u> <u>you</u>. The prospect or customer must "feel" that they need <u>you</u> more than you need them.

♥ ♥ ♥

Selling is Like the Ritual of Dating

This chapter leads us down a whole different hallway, if you will. **Now we're going to be talking more about the psychology behind marketing.** You see, selling is like the ritual of dating: the more you need them, the faster they run. **To really succeed as a marketer, you've got to let them come to you independently—or to at least *think* that they have.** The prospect must feel as if they need you more than you need them. Now, some people call that manipulation. Fine; I'm okay with that. You should be, too, if you have to think of it that way; **because otherwise, you're losing out on a lot of money that could and should be yours.**

I knew this guy years ago, when I was in my early twenties and I was out there chasing girls. He wasn't that good looking, but he did really well: he had women all over him. So I asked him, "What's your secret?" Well, he told me something I've never forgotten and that I hope you'll never forget: "All I do is take this back table." There was one bar that he and I went to, you see, and he said, **"I just take this back table, and I sit here. They all come to me."**

At the time, I thought he was a cocky egotistical bastard, and maybe he was. But I realize now that there was something to what he was saying, because the rest of us were chasing these women... and the more we chased them, the more they ran. And where did they run? They ran right to this guy, the guy with that attitude of, **"Hey! If you want to be with me, that's fine. If you don't want to be with me, that's okay too."**

There's some power it that kind of attitude. Although it's subtle, it's also very real. We recognize this in other things. **There are certain people who attract others, and there are people who repel others.** Part of that repulsion is that some people just try way too hard. Most people don't like that, so the more the repulsers try, the worse things are. On the other hand, some people are simply there: if you like them, that's great. They have no problem with you liking them. And if you don't like them, that's great, too. They have no problem with that, either.

If you ask 100 different marketing experts what marketing is all about, you're going to get 100 slightly different answers. If you put a roomful of marketers together, they'll argue about a lot of different points. **But one thing that almost all of them would agree on is that marketing is all about** *differentiation.* It's about being different from the next guy. **It's about being unique in ways that are important to your average prospect, especially the people you want to become your best customers.** It's those unique differences that are the "attractor factor," like the friend of mine from 30 years ago, back when I was a single guy.

While the rest of us were just making fools out of ourselves around all these young girls, this guy was just sitting back and waiting. To me it's a really great metaphor for business. **Dan Kennedy has a concept called "take-away selling," and what that's all about is putting it out there and pretending that you really don't need them as much as they need you.** Dan said that in the early years, when he was struggling financially, barely making it, just barely able to pay his bills, he used this method often. When a new client would call him up, or an old client that hadn't done business with him for awhile... even if his schedule was wide open, he would say, "Let me look at my calendar." And then he would put his phone down and come back in a little bit and say, "No, no. Next week is out. Sorry, the week after that is out too. But I *do* have one opening three weeks from now... No, actually I've got two openings. Three weeks from now we can make it on Tuesday the 14th, or we can make it on Thursday the 16th... And I might be able to slot you in on that Friday morning, in the 17th, maybe."

Think about that. The guy is practically starving, he desperately needs money, and he really wants to get the clients right then and there. **But he knows that the more the client senses that he's desperate, the more likely they are to run.** So *you've* got to be the one running; you can't be chasing, at least not in the perception of the client. The chaser has less power than the chased, in this scenario... **so never sound like you're too desperate.** People don't like that. Desperation is not an attractive quality. **What *is* attractive is when someone has something that you want.** *That's* attractive. People who just try to take, take, take from you, and are real desperate, and come across as needy... ugh, get rid of those people as fast as you can. You always need to have the opposite.

So all of your marketing, all of the communications you send out to your customer base, must come from a position of strength and power. That way, your customers are the ones who are chasing you, rather than vice versa. You don't want to seem like the desperate guy running around chasing anything that moves, saying, "I'm looking for anything! Anyone! Somebody pick me!" That's pretty much the kiss of death when you're looking for a date, and it's just as bad when you're looking for a customer. No one wants to feel like you picked them because you just had to have someone. **They want to feel special... and even more, they want to feel they've chosen you.** The person who tends to attract the opposite sex is the one who says, in a sense, "Whatever. I'm not seeking anybody. So if you want me, you know where to find me." That type of a person tends to attract more people, because they don't seem desperate. They're completely content with their situation.

So if you're a marketer and you look like you're desperate, if you look like you're running around trying to get anybody to respond... **well, that approach can backfire and have a negative impact on your business.** On the other hand, if you're a little elusive, if it seems like you're not seeking them out, if you're sort of just putting the offer out there and you seem like you don't really care whether they say yes or no.... That can have the opposite effect. **That can make people want to chase *you*. You're saying your offer probably isn't going to be for them... which is what makes it attractive to them.** There have been times in the past where we've told people, "Listen, we're going to send you your money back on this offer... so don't respond to it." And typically those people, when we try to talk them out of it, want it even more.

I've got a favorite line that relates to this concept, one that we've adapted from someone else. It goes like this: "Whether you respond or not, I'm going to be eating steak tonight." That kind of line just drips with this concept of indifference, or even arrogance. "Hey! Say yes, say no, doesn't make a difference to me. I'm doing fine either way. I'll be eating a nice juicy T-bone steak tonight no matter what." What that's saying to them is, "It's not going to bother me if you say no. In fact I'd rather you *did* say no, because that means I don't have to take your order and do the work." You don't say it like that, but that's the idea. **"Hey! It doesn't matter to me whether you say yes or no. I'm making this offer available to you. If you want to respond, great. If you don't respond, great. Whatever. You choose; it's not going to matter to me."**

That's the idea behind the message that you present. It's sa**ying, "Your order is not going to make or break me.** I'm not depending on you, so if you want to depend on me, that's fine. If you need me, that's great. But I don't need you." **Doing that will make your offer appear less desperate.** You don't want to go too far with this, of course, but you certainly don't want to go in the opposite direction. The real danger is that your sales message comes across as desperate, like you're looking for anybody and everybody who will buy. It sounds like you need customers so bad you don't discriminate. **That kind of message can backfire, because people will feel like you're so desperate that anyone will do, and that's a bit insulting.** Just like dating, if you're the one looking desperate, that's a turn off. On the other side of the coin, if you make it feel like you're not desperate, if you make it feel like you don't need them, **you'll find that they will chase you even harder.**

For example: if you tell them that an offer is limited and that there's a chance— probably a good chance—that

they're not going to be able to get in on it, they'll fight to be a part of it. Let's say there are only 23 of these things available, so you try to talk them out of buying; you act like, "If you buy this, it's going to be a hassle for me." If that's the tone behind your sales message, people will chase you harder for it. They'll kick down doors to get your offer.

In the past, when we've told people that there were just a few items available in the offer, we've had people FedEx us their order form. Now, why would someone pay $20 or $30 to overnight a single sheet of paper to us? They could have faxed it. **But they absolutely, positively had to get it here overnight, because the fear of missing out was so strong that they didn't want to take the chance of doing so.**

People will sometimes do crazy things when they're desperate to respond to your offer; and that kind of action lets you know that people are excited and want to do business with you. **So, you want to create an atmosphere that makes people want to do business with you, an atmosphere that makes it so that they're choosing *you* instead of having them feel like you're hunting them down.**

CHAPTER FOUR

The average business person spends their day *"putting out brush fires"*… Their time and energy gets zapped by all the minor problems that come up from day to day. They are <u>never</u> able to pull back and work on their businesses.

There is no real game plan or strategy!

Many people think they are running their companies — but all they are doing is running the day-to-day operations…

They are locked into survival.

Stop Putting Out Those Brushfires!

Instead of focusing on what's important, the average business person spends their entire day putting out brushfires. **Their time and energy gets zapped by all the minor problems that come up, and they're never able to pull back and work on their businesses the way they should.** There's no game plan for success. Many people think they're running their companies, but all they're doing is overseeing the day-to-day operations. And when they're doing that, they're just locked into survival mode... or they're asleep at the wheel. **The truth is, they might indeed be very busy — but there's no strategy behind their actions.** There's no way of trying to prioritize what's more important and what isn't important at all. **Often, they spend their time doing things that anybody else in their company could do.**

People who are really dedicated to making their businesses work should read the book *The E-Myth* by Michael Gerber. There's a concept that comes out of that book called working *on* your business rather than working *in* your business. That's what this principal is all about. **Focus on what matters, which are the things that only you can do.** Every single day, you've got to think about your marketing and the innovative strategies you're using to continue to develop your company, to make it more attractive in the eyes of the people that you want become your very best customers. You've got to have a plan. You've got to have a strategy. **You've got to do something *every single day***

that could significantly impact the bottom line.

Every single day you should spend time developing newer products and services for your customers, learning more about those customers, determining what it is they really want and what's going to get them excited the most. Keep thinking about the competition—who's doing the very best and why they're doing such a good job, and how you can incorporate all the various things you see working for others in your marketplace. These are the kinds of things that make the cash register ring.

Other tasks are better left for other people. I'm a big believer in delegation; if someone else can do the photocopying, let them. If you're not thinking about sales and profits every day, you're not thinking. Sales and profits are the lifeblood of your business; they're the oxygen. You've got to keep them moving constantly. **Anything that brings in more sales and profit is just too important to abdicate or delegate to somebody else while you're putting out the brushfires.** Most small business owners work very hard and still don't succeed—because they're locked into the day-to-day things. When all is said and done, they try to do everything except what they should *really* be doing. The work they're doing isn't making any real impact, because it's the kind of work that doesn't require any great skill or ability.

So think about this: what are the few things that you can do every day that no one else can to build your business and make more money? Again, it's about developing better products and services, better promotions that will get your customers and the prospective buyers in your market all jazzed up, things that keep people excited about your business, things that are *innovative*. **A business must constantly be in motion, because the market's always in motion.**

As I've mentioned before, we're getting ready to open this retail pet boutique. But we've never been in the retail business before, so when we got started, we bought all these books on retail success. In fact, *Retail Success* is the name of one of the books written by a consultant we're working with. **In any case, what we're looking for in all these books are the common denominators.** The retail stores that are doing the very best—what exactly are they doing? Simple question. In fact, it's the question that a lot of these authors try to answer in their books, and in the various consulting programs and services that they offer.

One of those common denominators turns out to be something that we do all the time, which is very pleasant and comforting for us to realize. **Our entire business is orientated around change.** In fact, that's something that Randy Hamilton, who's been with our company for over two decades, likes to say: "The product of M.O.R.E., Inc. is change." Why does he say that? Because we're constantly coming up with new, new, new. **There's always something new, something to get excited about, something to get fired up about, something to keep our customers coming back again and again.**

Well, is what we're offering *really* new? It is... and it isn't. **It's different, but in a sense it's the same.** It's all just variations on a theme—an endless theme of knowing what your customers want, and trying to give them more of it, so they always get the feeling when they come back and do business with you that there's going to be something different this time. **They never know what's going to be next; you're keeping people in suspense a little. You're doing things that are fun and exciting.**

All that takes thought and planning. It takes a lot of discipline. But it's all necessary: these are the few things that you *have* to do to get the biggest bang for your buck. **Doing these things will separate you from all those other business people who really don't own a business. What they own is a job**— and, it's the worst job in the world, too. It's a job that they're ultimately going to fail at, because they're going to get eaten up by the more aggressive competitors who *are* doing all the things I'm talking about here.

That's why you, as the business owner, can't be running around putting out brushfires. Now, you do have to be fully cognizant of the fact that every business has a wide variety of things that need to be done every day. A lot of people think only of the glamorous side of having your own business: the enjoyment of being your own boss, the ability to set your own hours, the freedom to go on vacation whenever you like. And where do people go with that ambition? They turn to things like franchises, retails stores, restaurants. They turn to things like home businesses, Internet businesses. And then they usually find that the dreams, the glamorous side of business, disappear in the reality of the day-to-day grind.

Consider someone who starts a retail store and spends 60-80 hours a week in the store, doing everything. They're running the cash register, they're trying to keep track of the books, they're answering the phones, they're trying to ship out orders that come in by mail or over the Internet. They're doing the taxes. They're doing payroll. They're ordering inventory. They're setting up the store. They're doing the cleaning. They're fixing the toilet when it goes out. They go buy bug spray, because they saw a cockroach the other day in the corner of the store. The computer's down right now, so they've got to fix it. They spent 45 minutes on the phone with tech support trying to get an answer because they can't figure out why, when you push this button, the cash register does something they don't expect.

Aargh! That's putting out brushfires! It's the day-to-day grind of the business and not so much the glamour, the reasons why people start businesses in the first place. So what happens is you have this situation where people want to be in business for themselves, but then the reality of it is a lot different and more difficult than they thought it would be, and they're wearing way too many hats, doing too many different things. **It wears them thin, and they're never able to actually work *on* their business and do the things that really bring business in.** So they never figure out how to bring in more customers. They never figure out how to write offers that get their existing customers to do more business with them.

There's no real goal except survival... and a lot of these people get burned out. Their businesses go under because of exhaustion. They can't cope. They end up going back to the workforce, doing what they were doing before they got into their business. The dream turns into a nightmare.

What they needed from the very beginning was a strategy for letting *other people* do all the small stuff, all the day-to-day things, while they focused on the marketing. I think about the business we have here, and the way that we work like a well-oiled machine. That doesn't mean things don't break down occasionally, but we've got a different department to handle each type of task. Now, we have 20 or so full-time employees, but it doesn't have to be that way. You can have a smaller operation and use the same kind of strategy.

We've got a department that handles data processing. That means when orders come in, the orders get processed, the credit cards get charged, the checks get deposited. They do all the administrative work to get orders processed and into the building where they belong. Then we have people who work in our shipping department so that orders that come in get shipped in a timely manner. We have a printing department for some of our printing (though some of it is outsourced). All the printing for all the orders gets done, and that gets processed and orders get shipped out.

After someone receives our order, they may have a question about something—so we have a customer service staff to help them through their questions and concerns. Of course, we have a sales and marketing department that's responsible for developing the offers we make to our clients, and sales people who take those orders. **The whole thing is in operation so that I and Chris Lakey and a few others can focus on the marketing. We're all here doing what we do best, and letting other people do what *they* do best.** It's a big operation full of many parts, all of them important to the whole game, the whole business of serving our customers and making a profit. I promise you, if Chris and I were to try to wear all those hats, our business would fail miserably, and it wouldn't have lasted nearly as long as it has. We're not good at the administrative side of business, which is why we have other people who do that well.

Putting out brushfires really is a problem that a lot of business owners have, because they're trying to do too many things. Now, sometimes there are brushfires that only the person at the top can put out; so you've got to tend to those. **But the day-to-day stuff, the daily operations, are for other people to take care of.** If your business has grass out front, you don't spend an hour mowing the grass yourself; you pay someone else 10 bucks to mow the grass for you. If you need a computer worked on, you hire a computer tech to come figure out what's wrong with your computer. Have someone helping you ship out products, so you're not sitting there 'til 10 o'clock at night boxing stuff up. In and of themselves these things may not be that big of a deal, but they add up to steal your time and energy. They can zap you of your resources mentally and physically.

Let other people spend their time putting out your brushfires. That's working smart, not just working hard. **When you hand off the brushfires to others, all your activities can be focused on your primary objectives.** You're getting more done, and you're getting the *right* things done.

CHAPTER FIVE

❧Creativity❧

The creative process is <u>not</u> neat, clean, or pretty. It is not organized. It is dirty, messy, disorganized, and chaotic! It is filled with taking all kinds of unrelated ideas — and <u>mixing</u> <u>them</u> together in a very special way. It is deciding to do something — <u>without</u> knowing how you are going to do it. And then figuring it out as you go!

Creativity is *Not* Neat, Clean, Or Pretty

Now, with direct mail as the theme, I want to talk about creativity. Creativity is an interesting subject in and of itself. Think about a young child; children are naturally creative. They live in this dream world, where they're absolutely open to everything: those minds are like little sponges. What happens, as we get older, is that we typically lose some of that creativity. **Now, creativity is a natural part of who we are. People somehow get the idea in their heads that they're not that creative, and then that belief becomes a reality, a self-fulfilling prophecy.**

Because they think they're uncreative, they tend to lose that creative edge.

The creative process is not neat, clean or pretty. **It's dirty, messy, disorganized and chaotic, like child's play.** It's filled with all kinds of unrelated ideas, which get mixed together in a special way. **It's deciding to do something, without knowing how you're going to do it, and then figuring it out as you go.** It's putting the why before the how. Everybody wants to know, "How am I going to do this, how am I going to do that?" Well, that's not the important part. The important part is setting the goal first.

Case in point: a recent Thursday afternoon. Most of the people M.O.R.E., Inc. work Monday through Thursday; for example, Chris Lakey works ten hours a day, Monday through Thursday. Me, I work seven days a week. So, we're having our end-of-the-week discussion, and I knew it was just a small opportunity to talk to Chris, because unless it's really important, I usually don't call him on the weekend. This week, I was trying to figure out a problem (a good problem). We've got an all-new direct mail package, and we started looking at what we had to do to reach our goal of doubling. We try to double our money on every promotion, you see; if a promotion costs us $1,000 bucks, we try to bring in $2,000 with it. That's our goal.

We use two-step marketing for direct mail, which means that in step number one, you generate the lead. Step number two, you follow up with the lead and convert the lead to the sale. **And so, in order to double our money on this particular promotion, we looked at getting 3% from our lead generation and converting 10% of those people.** That's a target only, because you never know what you're going to get — but you can't let that stop you from setting the goal. The goal was that we needed to hit 3% percent on the front-end, so for every 1,000 packages we mailed out, we needed to get 30 leads — 30 people to raise their hands and say, "Yes, send it to me."

And then, out of those 30, we needed three of those people to respond to our initial backend offer. At this point, we still don't know how we're going to do that. **See, you start with the why, or the goal, and then you figure out how to do it later. That's where the creativity comes in.** Some of the discussion Chris and I had that Thursday afternoon was about that, because it's not just about getting 30 people out of 1,000 to raise their hand; it's about getting 30 people that are well-qualified enough to raise their hands so that 10 percent of *those* people will immediately respond to Step Two.

You have to do those things; it's a formula. So we wrote down a bunch of ideas, I forgot about it, I ended my day, and **then the next morning I got up early to consider them.** I always try to get up about 5:00 o'clock in the morning or a little bit before, by the way — and sometimes I really have to force myself, because I realize that it's necessary and useful. I'm still tired, but I know that morning is magic for me. In fact, I think everybody has a period of time that's magic for them. It doesn't have to be morning: my friends Alan Bechtold, Michael Penland, and Don Bice are late-night guys. They like staying up until 3:00, 4:00 in the morning. That doesn't work for me. Five in the morning is my magic. It's a time where there are no distractions, and my wife is still in bed. **I don't have any responsibilities other than the projects in front of me.** After the first pot or two of coffee kicks in, it's a great thing for me; I just love it. (I can't imagine life without coffee. It's part of the creative process. To me, coffee and creativity go hand in hand.)

So after having this conversation with Chris on Thursday about how we were going to get 3% of the people to respond and then convert 10% on the back end, which is asking a lot in our market for what we're trying to do, I woke up Friday morning and I just started writing. **I wasn't even thinking about what I was writing. For me, part of the creative process is just opening the filters wide open.** Sometimes I'll do it on a legal pad where I scratch everything out, sometimes I'll do it on a computer; but the point is to stay open to everything and write down as many ideas as possible. **Part of the secret to getting**

good ideas is to get a *lot* of ideas. It took me years to learn that, too. You start off with a hundred ideas; then eventually, you narrow it down to the three or four that are best.

Creativity is a messy process. It's not neat and clean and pretty. **When I was considering this problem, I wrote down a whole bunch of ideas; I didn't try to second-guess any of them.** Sometimes, the crazier the idea, the better; just write it down. **Get it out of your brain; just stay open and receptive.** And then later, as I went along with the process, I ultimately came up with the "how" part of it... and the direct mail package ultimately got put together. But it was all based on things that started out as a conversation last Thursday afternoon.

And here's another thing as it relates to direct mail. A lot of the direct mail packages that you get are made to look like they're done from start to finish in one whole piece. They start with "Dear friend" and then launch into the text, which flows on until you hit the "Sincerely" and then the signature, which is sometimes followed by a "P.S." and all that. But they *weren't* put together like that. **What you have to realize is that any direct mail letter was created in little pieces, then stitched together using a format like the seven-step formula that I discussed earlier.**

It's a very creative thing. It's not always neat and clean; there's frustration and confusion all along the way. I feel like a lot of people want to avoid all that, so they avoid doing the kinds of things that create frustration and confusion. And yet, I believe firmly that in some ways, these things can be your friends — just as fear can be your friend, as long as you're not letting it stop you, as long you're using it as fuel rather than becoming vapor-locked. Frustration and confusion are part of every

52

promotion we've done in the history of our company. In the 22 years we've been in business, there's been a point during every promotion when I've said, "Oh my God, why did I even start this thing? Why?" **But that point has been short-lived every time. You get through it, figuring things out as you go. That's part of the creative process.**

There are a couple of dangerous things involved with this confusing creative process, and I've already revealed the first: that you don't even try. If you back off and don't move past your confusion the moment you become confused, you can stall. **The second danger is to think that other people are already more talented than you, or more skilled — so why should you even try?** My argument is that there are people out there who *want* you to think they're somehow special. A lot of the experts who do those marketing seminars want you to think that they have some natural gift, because they want you to then give them more of your money.

Well, I've had the privilege to get to know quite a few of these people; and it's been a wonderful privilege, because I've found that they're *not* superhumans. Sure, we call Eric Bechtold the "Young King Midas," for example, because it seems that everything he touches turns to gold. But part of that's just hype — because the fact is, the man works about 100 hours every week. And those 68 hours when he's supposed to be sleeping, he's dreaming about work, and he's thinking about work. He's just a man — but he's an amazingly hard-working man.

It all boils down to work and creativity in combination. I think that entrepreneurs can be very creative, whereas chief executives of big companies don't think that way. I believe that the analogy of comparing a new business to a baby, versus an adult, is quite valid here. **When your business is brand new, you get all creative and spend a lot of time thinking about creativity as it relates to your business.** How can you creatively bring in customers? How can you be creative as you're getting your business launched? And then, as that business develops and grows into a more established enterprise, the creativity tends to go away. You get mired down in the day-to-day, and you want to do things the fastest and easiest way... and so you lose a bit of your creative edge. Pretty soon the business is old and established, and maybe it's been taken over by a board of directors instead of that entrepreneur who started it. It's even further removed from that creative process that got it started, and things aren't really creative at all. **It just rolls along on momentum, and eventually it dies.**

The creative process, I think, really is the lifeblood of a business. Creativity is what drives innovation. It's people asking "Why not? Why can't we do something different? Why do we have to continue doing things the way we've always done things?" That kind of innovation especially drives technology. At some point along the way, someone asked, "Why can't we check our email on our cell phones?", and so today we have Smart Phones, which can do email and web browsing in addition to acting as phones. Before that, someone had to ask, "Hey, why can't we talk on a phone that's not connected to the wall?" Get my drift here?

Chris Lakey used to have what they called a "bag phone," one of the first cell phones that came in a bag and had a cord still, but the cord was attached to the bag. You zipped up the

54

bag and took it with you when you were ready to go. He had to plug it into the cigarette lighter in a car to power it. Sometimes, on TV, they still poke fun at these old cell phones. They were about a foot long and bulky.

At some point someone had to innovate and think, "Hey, let's see if we can make a mobile phone device that people can carry with them away from home, so they can answer the phone wherever they are." Bag phones were the result. And those early cell phones cost about 10 bucks a minute — you didn't want to ever talk to anybody on yours, you just wanted to show people that you *had* one.

My laptop computer is pretty thin, and yet it's not the thinnest on the marketplace. There's something called the MacBook Air that's paper thin; in the original commercials, they literally had people pulling them out of manila envelopes. Before that, the first laptops were an couple of inches thick, at least, and they generated a lot of waste heat. If you actually dared to put one on your lap, you'd get your lap burned! But the reason they existed at all was because someone thought, "Hey, why do we have to have a desktop at all? Why do we have to be tied down to a desk to use a computer? Let's have a mobile computer that we can take with us." And of course back then, you still had to plug it in to the wall to get an Internet connection... but now they're all wireless. **All these amazing advances in technology, and they all came from people saying, "Why not? Let's try something new. Let's think outside of the box. Let's be creative and let's innovate in the marketplace."** That happens all across the technology sector.

And that creativity, that innovation, is far from neat,

clean, or pretty. It's not organized. It's dirty, messy, disorganized and chaotic. People who tend to be structured, who tend to be neat, little boxed people — the creative process sometimes drives them nuts because it's messy. My desk, personally, is a mess: it's full of papers thrown all over the place and different projects I've got going on, and things I want to look at. It's a messy jumble of ideas and projects — and yet for me there's a kind of clarity there. And usually, when I throw something away is the minute that I realize I needed it, so I can't throw anything away.

In the creative process, there's a time when things come together; when you're working on a project and you've got all these scattered ideas, all these things you're working on, and then they start to take shape and transform, slowly, into the end product. You get to see the end result of all of the chaotic nature of the creative process. That's something you work toward along the way; but sadly, people often think that they have to have all that figured out in advance. Yet trying to bottle it up like that and get it perfect from the beginning can break you. **You end up losing some of that creative energy while thinking through how things are going to work, because you're so focused on how it's going to have to end.**

One of the things we do when we write sales copy is just let the ideas flow. You're not really trying to craft a sales letter at that moment; **you're just trying to get your thoughts and ideas on paper.** If you were to looked at a finished sales letter that we've written and you were then to see how it looked two weeks before that, you might not see many similarities at all. Sometimes a sales letter starts out 70 pages long, and at that point it's not really a sales letter; it's a collection of different chunks and segments strung together. There are ideas for headlines written up top, and you scroll down several pages and there are some notes about the offer and about "don't forget to add this in there" and "don't forget to put this part together." And then maybe you'll see some order form copy that needs to be worked on. All of these things are just scattered randomly: it's like a brain dump. **At this stage, you're just getting all your thoughts out and working on general ideas and concepts. As you refine it, it starts to look more like a sales letter.**

Now, I've never designed an actual physical widget, but I would imagine it's kind of that way when they develop the prototypes for new products. They probably have engineers sitting around working on mock-ups and drawings, and they see how these things go together, and pretty soon they've got a prototype, and it still doesn't work right... and when they try to get it to do what it's supposed to do, it smokes and it pops. Or it doesn't quite come out like it's supposed to, and then they keep working on it, and then pretty soon they have a prototype that really *does* what it's supposed to do, and they get it ready to go to the marketplace.

That creativity process is ugly in the beginning, but it gets more focused and neater as you move from the creative process towards the finished product. **And when it's done, you do it all over again. It's a constant state of having projects in different stages; some are always more done than others.** Some are nearly ready for the marketplace, some are at the beginning of the creative process, and there are others in all the stages in between. **If you're too focused on the end, you'll lose**

out on that process where you let your creative juices flow
and you're focused more on trying to get all the things that
you wanted out on paper.

A lot of people get bogged down in the details. That goes
along with the whole concept of why the "why to do" something
needs to come before the "how to do it." **The "how to do it" is
all in the details; the "why to do it" opens you up to lots of
different possibilities and keeps you focused on your goals in
general.** First comes the goal, the target; then you figure things
out as you go along. A lot of new products are developed this
way, we just don't know about it. Here's an example from the
music world: one of my favorite songs from when I was a
teenager made the band really famous at the time. Then, years
later, when I was reading a history of the band, I found out that
that famous song of theirs was actually three songs in one. They
had three different ideas, and they mixed them together and
created a hit song out of them.

Now, think about creativity as it relates to money. **The
whole money-making process is a very creative one,
especially for those people involved in the information
market.** People who sell informational products can, in a sense,
create it all out of thin air. But even in traditional brick-and-
mortar businesses, a lot of creativity is involved. Take our new
pet boutique. We're thinking up all kinds of cool, creative ideas
for that little business. That's part of what innovation is all
about. And as the late Peter Drucker once said, **everything in
business is an expense, except for two things: marketing,
which is all the things you do to attract and retain the largest
number of the best customers; and innovation, which is all**

about coming up with newer and better ways to do things — ideas that are outside of the box, creative business solutions that can make your business super-competitive.

There's a great book by David Schwartz called *The Magic of Thinking Big*. I'd recommend that book to anyone, although it's a little dated; it was written in 1959. Still, it changed my life when I read it. In that book, Schwartz talks about a business person who became extremely successful in, I think, the Atlanta, Georgia area. Years later, he was asked about what it was that transformed his business. And he said this: "At the same time every day, I close the door, unplug my telephone, and I sit down with a little pad and a pencil or pen. **And I ask myself: What can I do differently or better? What new ideas can I implement that will make the biggest impact on my business? I write down the ideas I have, and then I try to implement as many of those ideas as possible."**

So here's a simple idea: **just spend a little time every day thinking about how you're going to improve your business.** There's nothing too earth-shattering about that idea, and yet the truth is, very few people do this consistently. They do it sporadically at best, and probably a lot of people don't even do it at all.

As with lots of other things in life, if don't use your creativity, you lose it. Now, they say you stop being creative after the age of 40 — which is the biggest lie I've ever heard. There are plenty of people older than that who are razor sharp, and they get more creative by the year. One of them is our friend, Don Bice. Don isn't very sensitive about his age, like some of our other friends are — so he won't mind me saying that he's now in his 70s, and he's growing more creative every year. When you talk to him on the phone, he sounds like a man half his age.

Like anything else, creativity takes time and work and focus, so think about what David Schwartz said about the man who locked himself in his room with the phone unplugged so he could spend creative time with himself. **But don't just think;** *do.* This idea makes sense to all of us, and yet to actually do it on a consistent basis is the hard part. **So we put it off, and our businesses stagnate as we get older.** At one time they were very successful, but then we quit doing those things that made them successful to begin with — which was to engage in a lot of that innovative, creative thinking. **If you let that go, the business just goes away after a while and is eaten up by all of the other younger, more aggressive, more creative, more innovative businesses.**

The key here is to never lose that hunger and the creativity that got you started in business in the first place. Whatever you did in the beginning, as a young entrepreneur, you've got to continue to do. You've got to keep the hunger alive and keep the fire and energy going, and not get stuck in the doldrums — don't get stuck doing the same thing over and over again, unless of course those things work and are profitable. **Always be innovative, always be creative, and try to stay on the cutting edge of your marketplace.**

My best advice is to find that time of day that's magic for you, and then make it almost like a religion to spend that time working on the business, rather than *in* **it.** Keep trying to come up with as many ideas as you can to keep things moving forward in a fresh and positive way.

CHAPTER SIX

Roll-Out To Mega-Wealth!

The same strategy that generated $1,000.00 can be rolled-out to generate $100,000.00 **if** the market is big enough — and other factors can be closely matched.

Roll Out to Mega-Wealth!

One of the smartest marketing guys that I ever had the privilege to be around once told me that the secret to making millions of dollars is just to be able to make a thousand dollars. **In fact, he took it further: ultimately, his deal was that if you could make *one* dollar, you could make millions.** That statement has stuck with me for years. **What he was saying was, if you do things correctly in this business, you never have to risk very much at all.** You start by testing everything on a small basis. By doing small tests, you're able to determine what works and what doesn't. **When you find something that gives you a small profit, something that resonates with the target market, that's when you invest heavily and roll it out big-time — so you can create mega-wealth.**

You can test all kinds of ideas in a small way, for next to nothing. I came across this idea early on. I grew up in Great Bend, Kansas, which is just 90 miles down the road from Goessel. Great Bend is an oil field town, and when I was a kid I worked in the oil field. I did a lot of work in the oil fields when I was a teen, but my first job was in an oil field supply store, and I got to meet all these drillers. I was a kid and they liked me, and I liked them. They were just good old boys that I befriended, and they told me how the oil business worked. It's so simple that it's not even funny. **You see, they drill all these different wells, and maybe only one out of 10 actually hits.** But mainly the drillers do it on other people's money. The drillers sell leases, and the drillers always own just a little piece of it, so that they never actually have to pay for much.

Most of the time when they drill for oil or gas, nothing comes up but maybe salt water. They call that a dry hole. But all they have to do is hit on one out of 10 to profit, or even just one out of 15. When that one well comes in, they can make some serious money, depending on the price of oil and other critical factors, including the cost of production in getting it out of the ground. I think this is a good metaphor because it's just another way of rolling out to mega-wealth. **You test to see what you come up with, and invest heavily in that one big strike.** That's how the same strategy that generates $1,000 can be rolled out to generate $1,000,000, if the market is big enough and if other factors can be closely matched.

And when I say other factors, I'm talking about other factors within the tests you did. **So you test everything on a small basis, and then, assuming that there's enough interest, you move forward in a big way.** Let me give you some examples from M.O.R.E., Inc. I mentioned in an earlier section of this book that as of this writing, I was recently talking to Chris Lakey about a new direct mail package that needed to be put together. We were looking at certain percentages of response as our target goals. And then, over the next few days, I worked on it steadily.

As we were doing the seminar that this portion is based on, my graphic artist was faxing over some pieces from that project to our fulfillment company, the people who take care of making and copying our DVDs and CDs. They fulfill the orders that come in from our initial advertising and lead generation, which represents a test for us. We don't know if it's going to work or not; it's like drilling for oil. We know where our "oil" ought to be — there's some science to that — **but we can't guarantee anything, so we have to test to see if we'll actually make a strike or not. Only then do we go through the expense of deepening that hole and extracting out of it every dollar we can.**

I used to work a seismograph crew when I was a kid; that was a fun job. We used to drill deep holes and throw dynamite into the holes. Then, when it exploded, the seismographs in the ground would measure how the shockwaves propagated through the ground. If things looked good for oil, then they drilled in the area — but not until then. It's a lot cheaper to do seismograph tests than to drill for oil. **It's not an exact science, but it's better than throwing money away on guesses.**

Our business is like that. **You know, in general, the things that your market will respond to and what they won't respond to, based on past results — marketing seismograph tests, if you will.** And then you do these little tests like the one that we're doing next week (as of this writing), based on the direct mail package I just finished up yesterday afternoon. We're going to send about 10,000 packages to what we call the "outside lists." Those are people outside of our own customer base. There are millions of these people out there, so it's like drilling for oil. We're going to do that 10,000-person test, and we're going to see if it's a dry hole — or if we hit a gusher. **If we get the numbers we want, if we make money on that little tiny test, then we'll roll it out big-time.** And if we can roll it out consistently, we can make a boatload of money.

Right now we do a lot of what we call new customer acquisition mailings — that is, mailings to people who have never done business with us before. We're mailing 40,000 pieces a week on that. **So if that little 10,000- piece mailing works, we can roll it out to the customer acquisition level, and it could potentially be worth many hundreds of thousands of dollars a month to us.** But it costs us relatively little if the test fails... and remember, we just need to get three out of a thousand people to become one of our customers. That's our minimum goal. But if the idea works, we can roll it out big.

It's a really exciting principle, because you can also test aggressively. You can come up with wild and crazy ideas and see if they resonate. Your tests are only limited by your imagination, really, which is both good news and bad news — because if you have a lot of imagination, you have more choices, whereas your choices are limited if you're unimaginative. **But still, you can test all kinds of weird ideas but only spend just a little bit of money on the actual test.** And then, if it works, you can roll it out and potentially make millions of dollars.

The people who make the most money consistently in this business are the ones that test the most. It's just like in the oil business: the drillers who are out there drilling as many holes as they can are going to make the most money. If they only hit on one out of 10 holes and they drill 100 holes, that means they've got 10 winners. If they only drill 10, they've only got one winner. So ideally, you test as much as you can, testing a lot of small things, so if something doesn't work you're only losing that little bit of money you put into it. **If you do things right**

and think things through carefully, you can potentially lose money on nine out of every 10 or even 19 out of every 20 ideas and still make a profit.

So if you come up with all these ideas and have failure after failure — you lose all your money on this one, half your money on that one, 60% of your money on a third — all you need is one big winner to pay off all those dry holes. Rolling out that winner to the tune of hundreds of thousands or millions of dollars to the larger market may make you ten or a hundred times the amount of your investment, or even more. **Most failed entrepreneurs just go out there and test two or three things; and if those things don't work, they give up.** In so doing, they're losing out on money that could potentially be theirs if they'd just keep testing.

Incidentally: **once you get a decent customer list put together to roll out to, your risk factor goes way, way down.** Here's what I mean. We've been in the business for 22 years now, and we're up in the high 8,000s on our number of mailings. And that's just since we've been numbering them — probably only 13 or 14 years. **In all that time, we've lost money maybe three or four times when we mailed to our own customer list after testing items with them.** Why is that? Because our customers know us, they like us, they trust us; and when people know you and like you and trust you, they tend to be more receptive to your ideas. The response rates are much higher.

We also use our customer base as a testing ground. If our customers get really excited about something, we know that there are potentially millions of other people outside our customer base whom may be interested, too. These are people very like our customers; they've just never done business with us yet, though they may be on all these other mailing lists. **So if you're looking for a way to do a lot of testing without risking a single penny, in a way that you almost always make money, always test to your best customers first.**

It all starts with thinking of your customer base as a triangle or pyramid, with those best customers at the top. You need to segment or prioritize those folks so you know who they are — and that prioritization can be done in different ways. But you should know who your smaller group of best customers are. **If you test every offer to that smaller group of people first, it doesn't cost you that much money.** And after a while, through experience, you'll know what they're most excited about, and so you just start rolling those kinds of things out to them. When you do it that way, you lose very little money — if you know what you're doing, and if you're smart about it. **You can test a whole lot of different offers this way, to find those few that you can roll out and make a lot of money with.** Of all the strategies I've learned over the years, I can't think of a more risk-free way to make money.

But this method still requires you to test as many different things as you possibly can. And let me highlight the fact that **it's important to always start small.** Too often, people have these grandiose goals of making millions of dollars or otherwise being super-successful, and they think really big. They're overlooking the possibility of starting slowly when they do that. It's important to have big goals, but they get over-focused on the big dreaming and miss the more modest possibilities. It starts with a small idea; and as I've often said,

"A big shot is just a little shot that kept on shooting."

I think it has to be that way with testing. **You test small; and then a successful test becomes a main offer, and then that offer becomes an offer that you continue rolling out to everyone, until it becomes super-successful.** Our new customer acquisition process — that is, what we do to get new customers and to maintain what we call a front-end marketing plan — goes something like this. We'll start out with an idea for a product, and we'll create an offer that we're going to mail to a small group of our best customers. Sometimes we try things that are a little questionable; in other words, some ideas are really good, and we have a really strong belief that they'll be successful, whereas some we're a little less sure about.

If we're not sure, we'll develop an offer and mail it to a small number of our best customers. That number could be as small as 1,000 or 2,000 (which really is a small number to us). **If we feel really good about the offer, we might try it with 5,000-10,000 of our best customers.** And then we'll wait to see how it works, how they respond to it. We rarely lose money mailing to the customers on our preferred mailing list. **If they don't respond well, then there's a good chance nobody else will either.** But if it works there, we'll test it to a bigger group of customers.

So let's say we mail 5,000 pieces for a brand new offer, and it gets a good response. If that's the case, we'll mail it to more of our best customers — maybe the rest of the customers on our preferred customer list — and we'll wait for those results to come in. **As they do, we'll monitor those results to see if it looks like it's going to work; if not, we'll try to figure out**

why. Generally, if we make it work to a small group of our best customers, the rest of our best customers will also respond in similar numbers. If that happens, we release it to our entire customer list. The next step is offering the product or service to an outside list of people who don't know us, people we don't already have a relationship with.

Well, do you think that just because our customers responded well that we'll immediately try to make a million dollars from that campaign? No way! What we do is test small again. **We've rolled out to a small group of our best customers, and then the rest of our customers, and *then* we start on the outside list with a small test.** We might mail 1,000 or 2,000 pieces, or sometimes 5,000 pieces, to new prospects. If that works, we'll probably test a second time, with another few thousand people. **And if *that* goes well, and we make a good profit on that, we'll roll it out to a bigger audience.** This can be a long process, taking as much as six months, which is why a lot of people don't like to do it. Eventually, though, we might examine the records and say, "It looks like we have a winner here." **And then the offer becomes what we consider our front-end control piece, which is something we mail on a weekly basis.** If it's the right offer, we might mail as many as 40.000 pieces of mail a week, promoting that offer to acquire new customers.

All of that is done in a very calculated way, starting small. We're never going to make a million dollars with one new mailing. We make the big money on a promotion by starting with small tests, and then continuing to retest, and rolling it out to more and more customers, and then eventually finding an offer that works with new customers. **So it's a systematic approach that takes time, especially if you want to reach the broader marketplace.** Sadly, a lot of people don't test at all, for whatever reason, and I think that's foolish. Yes, sometimes it gets really frustrating to test and test, and have things not go right. You spend a lot of money and a lot of time and energy trying to come up with new ideas, new ways to present your offer so that you get more people to respond — so it can be frustrating to roll out a bunch of offers and have them flop.

But by testing a lot of ideas, you find out which things work best, and you're able to more quickly get your product to the main marketplace beyond your customer list. We don't do this now as often as we should, but many times in the past, we've tested five or ten different versions of the same sales letter or offers; all that's different is the way we're presenting it. **Maybe it's as simple as using a different envelope or a different order form, or a different free gift, or something like that — but it's the same basic offer.** We'll test those all at once and see which has the best response. Within 6-8 weeks, we know which of those five or ten variations works best in general. That allows us to quickly roll out the offer to more people, and we know which of the ideas we want to retest.

When you're using this strategy of rolling out to mega-wealth, you can test confidently, because you're testing small numbers of pieces. **The cost to test 1,000 pieces of direct mail isn't very much, compared to the lessons you can learn from doing that.** If all you ever do is mail your offers out to big groups of people, you're never going to be able to get the feedback that's valuable to your business and that's necessary to help you grow.

It's just about starting small. And yes, your goal in everything you do is to make a lot of money, and you want to stay focused on that more abstract goal. But the way you accomplish that goal is through all this smaller testing that you do to find out which results are going to be the most promising for you. **So start small, always test a lot, and then roll out those things that are most successful — and that will help you achieve the end goals that you're trying to accomplish.**

When somebody once asked Albert Einstein how he worked, he said, "I grope." Groping means feeling around clumsily; you're searching for answers, trying to feel your way through something. When you test a lot of ideas to the same general groups of people, you're groping. **Oh, you have a good idea of what to offer and what people are looking for; but the feedback you get helps you refine your ideas.** Some of the feedback is good, some less so. But it all comes together to give you an intuitive feeling of what works and what doesn't, and then you simply try to do more of what works and less of what doesn't. **You let the numbers tell you what to do.** The longer you're in the game, the more testing you do, the more you have that intuitive feeling of what the market likes and dislikes — but you need to understand those numbers.

CHAPTER SEVEN

☞ THE HAND ☜

Every offer or promotion must meet these five crucial steps:

1. Is it the right offer?

2. Is it going to the right person?

3. Through the right media?

4. With the right hook?

5. And does it fit together with some kind of long-term plan?

There are only a handful — but they're vital. This lets you focus on the essentials.

(I borrowed this hand concept from *Bill Graham*, the greatest rock-n-roll promoter who ever lived! Bill had his 'handful' of ideas he used for every major event. This let him do BIG THINGS and make quick decisions. It will do the same for you, too!)

The Hand

I got this idea from Bill Graham, the famous rock-and-roll promoter who died in the late 1980s. In Graham's day, there was nobody better. He was the very first music promoter who started doing football stadiums—the big concerts, the ones with 70,000, 80,000 people. Graham built an entire industry on that. In his wonderful book *Bill Graham Presents,* he offers the concept of the "Hand." For every single concert that Bill ever did—and he did thousands of them—he had five different things that he called his "Hand." It was a shortcut strategy for him, to simply try to figure out the five critical items for every concert he promoted. **The Hand let him see where the problems were; it let him quickly make decisions. I loved that concept so much that I've adapted it to DRM.** So there are five things that we're going to talk about on our Hand.

Before I reveal them, though, I want to say this: we started working with Russ von Hoelscher in the late '80s. Russ used to come to our home outside of Goessel, and he would spend the weekend helping us with our promotions. Actually, he more than helped us: he pretty much just did them for us. Oh, we gave him ideas; we brainstormed. It was great fun, a great learning experience. **But from the time I saw Russ do it, *I* wanted to do it.** I wanted to be able to take those ideas, put them on paper, and then move them through the entire process myself.

3 STEPS TO INSTANT PROFITS!

What Russ did back then was all by hand. Whenever he came in on a Friday afternoon to spend the weekend working with us, we would have these giant stacks of legal pads and a whole bunch of pens ready, and we would make sure we had lots of coffee, donuts, and stuff like that—lots of sugar and caffeine. **Then we would talk about all these ideas for promotions that we could do for our customers.** Russ would get excited, and when he got excited, Eileen and I would shut up and just let him go. He would start writing furiously, and then he would stop, and we would drink a little more coffee and talk a little more until Russ got excited again, and then all of a sudden he would start writing, and we would start shutting up.

At the end of the weekend, when we took him back to the airport on Sunday, we would have this huge stack of what had once been blank legal pads; but now they were full of Russ' scribbles. We would take them to the typist, she would type them up, and we would work the information it into a sales letter. **Then we would send it out to our customers and make lots of money.** It's a very simple business, really.

Well, I always wanted to do all that myself. I always thought, "Man, how cool is that? To be able to take ideas, put them on paper, send that paper out, and have people send you money! It's wonderful!" The thing that used to bother me, during the first seven or eight years that I was trying to learn what Russ did naturally, was that I had a lot of failures along the way. **It took me a long time to get it right.** I'm not the smartest guy, you see; I know I keep saying that, but it's true. The more you know me, the more you'll realize that I wasn't blessed with a high IQ. I envy those that were. So it took me seven or eight years to do what Chris Lakey did in seven or eight months... **but I finally learned it.** And the thing that used to bother me was that Russ would look at some of my early ideas for mailings, and he would say, "That won't work, " and I would get so angry. I'd worked so hard on these mailings, and when I sent or faxed then to him, he would just reply, "It won't work. It won't work. It won't work."

And frankly, I hate critics. Anybody can be a critic. It doesn't take any special talent to just criticize any idea: "Oh, that's bad." "That sucks." "Ha, forget that." **What takes talent is coming up with the ideas in the beginning: the optimism, the courage, the audacity to go out there and make it happen.** But what I didn't realize was that Russ wasn't being overly critical; he knew what he was talking about, that's all. **He knew it wouldn't work because it was missing certain key elements, and that's what this Hand of mine is all about!** These are the five key critical ingredients that every great direct mail or direct response ad must contain.

The irony is that now that I've been in the business for 22 years, when people bring me their sales letters, I do the same thing that Russ did... only I'm nicer about it, I hope. I don't just say, "Oh, that sucks," or "That's terrible," or whatever. I'm too much of a people pleaser to do that—**but I *can* instantly tell that it's not going to work, because it doesn't have these ingredients.**

And here they are: **the right offer, going out to the right person, through the right media, with the right hook, according to the right long-term plan.** The first four are the most critical; so let's talk about those four, and then we'll talk about the fifth as it applies to the whole formula.

As I've said before, we don't really sell products and services; what we really sell are offers. **An offer involves the product and service, but it also involves all the other stuff that goes along with it: the free bonuses, the guarantee, the call to action, etc.** The offer is everything that you're proposing to give to people in exchange for the money you're asking for. Think about those old Ginsu Knife commercials, or any infomercials really. Think of the way that they do things in those infomercials: "You'll get this. Plus, you'll get this. Plus, you'll get this. *Plus*, if you act now, we'll give you this, and this, and this. And for a limited time…" It's like they don't stop! They just keep going on, and on, and on, until finally there's a huge package, and you find out that it's all for one easy payment of $19.95! Wow! They're making you an offer: that's what an offer is. You keep building it and building it, throwing in all kinds of other stuff.

So, first, it has to be the right offer. **That right offer has to go out to the right person; that's critical.** If you're getting zero response on something, the first thing you need to do is to be sure it's not going out to the wrong group of people. The right offer for one person is often the absolute wrong offer for another, you see.

Those are the first two fingers of the hand. **Next, it has to go out through the right media.** Direct mail is our favorite medium; but your best medium could be an ad in a national magazine, or it could be TV or radio, or a mix of all those and more. How are you going to get that sales message out there? **What's the best delivery vehicle?** Some media are wrong simply because they reach the wrong type of market; in fact, that's the number one reason they're wrong. You have to be very careful about that. Otherwise, something may be the wrong medium because it's too expensive, in which case you have to find something cheaper.

Then number four: the right hook. The hook is a little harder to explain than our other fingers of the Hand. We had Russ von Hoelscher with us on the phone a while ago, and he told use something interesting about his new program: "I'm writing so many of these commission checks every week, my wrist is hurting." *That's* a hook. **That's something that people will connect with and remember.** Jeff Paul, out of Chicago, made millions of dollars with an ad where the hook was, "I'm at home making money in my underwear." That's something that sticks in people's minds: Jeff Paul at home in his underwear. It's dumb, it's emotional—but you remember it.

In a current promotion for our Direct Pay System, part of our hook is that we're asking people, "Are you getting all of the money that you could and should be getting from these companies you're involved with?" It's something that's designed to stick in their heads, so they can remember it. **A hook has to be something unique; it needs to be an emotional, noteworthy thing.** The more you study other people's sales material and promotions, the more things will stand out for you. Then you'll be able to come up with ideas on your own, based on what you see other people doing. This direct pay thing—we keep talking about, "People send their checks directly to you." That's a kind of hook, because it's one of the things that people won't forget. **And again, it has to be the right hook, which**

means something to the person you're communicating with.

Then, number five: if it doesn't fit together with the right long-term plan, then you really shouldn't do it. This isn't gambling; this is a business. For example, you definitely need to keep and maintain the names and contact info of all your customers, so they become part of your mailing list and you can do other things with those people. Make it the basis of your overall game plan, then apply these other four hooks.

There are only a handful of elements here, and yet they're vital; **they help you make quick decisions, focusing on what really matters in your sales copy.** They're shortcuts, and they tell you what's right with your copy, and what's wrong. Recently, for instance, I wrote a really good sales letter for the wholesale printing club I've already mentioned a few times. I just loved that copy, but there was one problem: it didn't have an offer in it. Whoops! **Everything else was good, and I did a great job of presenting the whole concept, but didn't give people a reason to respond. That's part of what an offer is.**

Having a checklist like this, and knowing what's most important, will help you see any mistakes before they occur. That's vital for success. Consider aviation checklists, for instance. A seasoned, veteran pilot works through a takeoff checklist every single time, even if they're taken one of those big birds up into the sky thousands of times before. They go through it religiously, even though they probably don't have to. Probably, nothing bad would happen if they *didn't* go through their checklist... but God forbid they should miss one thing on their checklist one time, because it could mean their life, and everybody else's life along with it. **So checklists are**

important; and it's also important to know that there are formulas, common denominators, things you can point to in every business practice. Again, there's some risk involved; there's always some risk involved in business, **but it's** *calculated* **risk** if you know the formulas and strategies that keep businesses afloat.

It's been a while, but many of you will remember the name "Captain Sully." That's the name of the pilot who landed his commercial airliner on the Hudson when it was going down; he saved the lives of everybody onboard, and became a national hero. I remember hearing an interview with him, and he was trying to downplay the whole thing by saying, "I just did what I was trained to do." Exactly! He had seconds to react, and it became instinct for him when he recognized that the plane wasn't going to make it where it to was supposed to go, that he was going to be landing it in the river. Instinct took over, he did what he was trained to do, and he landed the plane safely on the water. The reason that happened for him was because of his training, the formulas and checklists that he had internalized over the years. I suppose it's probably similar to a war situation, where someone has been trained over and over again to behave a certain way, and to do a certain thing when this or that occurs. **It becomes instinctual.** You go into battle, and all of a sudden all of the training takes over, and you know what you're supposed to do.

Earlier, I mentioned about how when I was new at this, Russ von Hoelscher would tell me, "That won't work. That won't work, either." I questioned it then; but now I know that it's easy for an experienced direct mailer to spot what will and won't work, because we've been trained in how to spot a good offer, how to spot a good sales letter, and how to spot a good product. That comes as a natural ability of being a trained marketer. This strategy of the Hand, the five things here, was developed as the result of years of studying good DRM... so, these things play off a lot of other things. These five main points are based on, and distilled from, hundreds or thousands of different marketing strategies and principles that we've learned over the years.

Note that all five of these points have the word "right" in them: the right offer, to the right person, through the right medium, with the right hook, coupled to the right long-term strategy. There's many a wrong way to do things, you see; you could have the right offer, but send it to the wrong person, and this formula wouldn't work. **It's not enough to just have a good offer, it has to be the *right* offer to the *right* person.**

If you're using the wrong medium—even if you're trying to reach the right person with the right offer—you'll fail, or at least you won't be as successful as you could be. **And without the right hook, you'll also have less success than you should.** That's hard to quantify, however; it's easier to see it when you know what you're looking for, when you recognize it. **All these things really do go together like all the fingers on your hand.** Although you can survive without one finger, and many people do, they all serve a purpose—starting with that right offer.

What are you doing to get people to respond? We don't necessarily talk about a product here, because again, the product is secondary to the offer. **Many times, people will respond to the right offer, even if the product isn't necessarily superior.**

Think about a state fair, if you've ever been to one. They've got all those booths where they're selling all kinds of products and services. If you really, really stop and think, "Do I need this product?" the answer is, no, probably not. And the product may even not be that great—and yet they wrap it around a great offer, and they're up there pitching it in an effective way. They're using a microphone or headset, and they've got the speakers out on their table, and they're demoing the product and talking all about it. There's an energy and excitement there, as they're telling you all about the product and the benefits you're going to get. Maybe they're even letting you try it out yourself.

And then they tell you what their offer is, and today, it's a state fair special! Today, you can pick one up for just $19.95. But wait, we're going to give you a *second* one when you order today. And you notice they already have them packaged in sets of two in the back here, so when you say you want one and you get one free, all they do is reach back there and grab your set and hand it to you. Oh, and then they're also going to throw in this other dandy little thing here. Normally, it's a $19.95 value, but it's free today—and yes, they've got it boxed up in the same set back there.

That's the offer they've made, and it gets people to buy even if they weren't necessarily inclined to do so. It's not like they were on their way to Wal-Mart to buy that product; it just happens to be that there was a buzz created when they were making an offer and presenting that offer to you in that setting. **So the right offer is important; it's what you're doing to really get people to respond... but only the right people, of course.**

3 STEPS TO INSTANT PROFITS!

Previously, we talk about mailing lists being so important; and when you're doing direct-response marketing by mail order, **mailing lists of the right people are especially important.** You can have a really strong offer, and a really good product... but if it's being made to the wrong person, they're not going to buy. If they're not interested in your product or the kinds of offers you're making, it doesn't matter how good the offer is. **So when you're picking mailing lists, it's vital to work with a reputable list broker.** One of the worst things that can happen is that you're sending your offer to a person who's not inclined to buy, **so make sure that you rent the right buyers' mailing lists.** There are a lot of compiled lists on the market, where you can purchase the contact information for millions of households, but they're not a good idea for you. **They need to be targeted.** You need to know that they've already bought things similar to what you're offering.

With compiled lists, there's nothing that makes them inherently interested in what you have to offer, no matter what you offer. **Whereas if you buy a list of people who have bought opportunities like yours by mail, you know that that's a good list.** That doesn't mean your offer is going to be successful; it just means you're reaching the right kinds of people, those who are most likely to be interested in what you have.

And again, the right media. Are you choosing to advertise by mail, are you on TV, are you on radio, are you in the newspapers? What are you using to reach that marketplace? Where are you advertising, and what method are you using? Are you using a sales letter, are you using an audio CD, or are you using a website?

Add that to the right hook: the angle, the twist, the story —"making money in your underwear" —that kind of thing. Something that makes people remember you, makes people interested. **It's an angle; it's just something you're doing to get people to pay attention to you**—like the hook in the fishing analogy. If you have your bait, if you're using an artificial lure, is that hook interesting to the fish? Is there something on the hook that's going to make a fish want to bite... or is it a boring lure? A nice, shiny hook with a nice shiny lure on it will catch a fish. A boring piece of bait or boring lure won't. Maybe they're not interested in it; maybe it's not glittery enough or something. And hey, the concept of the hook isn't just used in the marketing game. The movie business and the music business use the hook too. It's something that's catchy, something that people will remember, something people will talk about, something that they'll sing to themselves, if it's a song.

Now: once you have all that in place, the fifth element is fitting them together with the right long-term plan. I think it's important for you to remember your ultimate goal here. Whatever you're selling right now, whatever your main thing is, it's probably not going to last forever. **Offers don't stick around.** People stop responding to them for whatever reason; your response rates will drop. It's built on something where the market changes, and people don't respond to that kind of product or offer anymore.

Your ultimate goal is to build a customer list, a list of people who buy from you again and again, in order to build a lifelong business and income for yourself. With that goal in mind, the products you sell, the offers you make—they're all just part of the goal of building a customer list, of getting people to do business with you repeatedly. The products may change, the methods may change, the market and the media may change—all those things can change, but you're still working toward serving a marketplace and providing them value and getting them to not only do business with you the first time, but getting them to continue doing business with you over and over. **So the fifth thing is figuring out where you're going and what your goals are; and once you do that, everything else becomes a part of trying to do the right things to accomplish that goal.**

CHAPTER EIGHT

Great Quotes:

"People are silently begging to be led."

— Jay Abraham

"You can learn more from movement than meditation."

— Gary Halbert

"It doesn't have to be good — just good enough."

— Dan Kennedy

"All it takes is just one idea to make a million dollars!"

— Russ von Hoelscher

"We sell to creatures of emotion — bristling with prejudice — and motivated by pride and vanity."

— Dale Carnegie

Take Heed of these Great Marketing Quotes

Let's take a break from our standard chapters to look at some marketing quotes that I believe define our field. I've alluded to some already, or mentioned them in other contexts. This first one is a good example. It's from Jay Abraham, probably the most expensive consultant in the world: I think he charges $5,000 an hour. What Jay says is that **"People are silently begging to be led."**

"People are silently begging to be led." They want to be told what to do. They're looking for direction. From a marketing standpoint, the best salespeople are the ones who are the most confident. They project that confidence, and people respond it; it helps them know what they need to do. **Also, in all your promotions, you have to *literally* tell people exactly what you want them to do, and how they should respond.**

Number two, from the late, great Gary Halbert: **"You can learn more from movement than meditation."** So many people want to just sit around, hoping that the right idea will come to them. Well, it won't. **The right idea comes to you when you're in the process of moving forward, testing a lot of different things, trying a lot of different things, learning what works, learning what doesn't work.**

The third quote is from one of my mentors, Dan Kennedy, who helped my wife and I a great deal back in the '90s. One of the things Dan says is, **"It doesn't have to be good, just good enough."** Part of the reason Dan says that is because **people tend to be perfectionists.** Just get it out there; it doesn't have to be perfect. "It doesn't have to be good, just good enough."

The fourth quote comes from Russ von Hoelscher. Russ told me this in 1989, when we first met him. We picked him up at the airport and we were driving back to Goessel, talking about this wonderful business of DRM. Just in conversation, he said to us, **"All it takes is one idea to make a million dollars."** At that time, we hadn't even made that much yet. It was shortly afterward that we came up with one idea that actually *did* make us over $1 million. So, just think about that. I would amend that a little to say, **"All it takes is one good idea, well-executed, to make $1 million."**

Then, last but not least, is a quote from the late Dale Carnegie, a truly great man. Dale said, **"We sell to creatures of emotion, bristling with prejudice, and motivated by pride and vanity."** I love that quote, because we *do* sell to people's emotions. It has always been that way, and it *will* always be that way. That will never change. **People buy for emotional reasons.**

Lately, I've been reading a lot of quotes from motivational websites. Here's one from John F. Kennedy that I like. Now, let me set this up for you: in the Chinese language, they use pictographic characters for their writing, and often those characters are made up of two root characters. So for example, in their calligraphy, you often have one word on top of another word, and that makes up a symbol that means something different. **JFK said that in Chinese, the word "crisis" is actually composed of two characters—one that represents** the word "danger," and the other that represents the word "opportunity."

When most of us think "crisis," we think of adversity. We think of challenges. I think it's interesting that the Chinese word for crisis represents two words, danger and opportunity. **Because it's so true: where there's adversity, where there's a challenge, there's also an opportunity for growth or for experiencing breakthroughs.** The thing about the strategies we use to accomplish success is that **they're just theories until you put them into practice.** So I think that it's important for everybody to just get out there and do it.

Don't just read my discussions of these things. **Put them into practice, and start to use them, because that's where you'll find your own breakthroughs.** When you put these things into practice, they will become a part of your life experience, instead of just something you read about. It's one thing to have a lot of experience by way of reading about something, or by way of gaining head knowledge. I would suspect that you, the reader, already have a lot of head knowledge. You've read stuff we have written. Maybe you get our newsletter, or you listen to our audio programs. You know a lot of stuff… **but until you transfer that knowledge into action, it's not worth a lot.**

Knowledge unapplied doesn't pay any bills. Knowledge unapplied doesn't get any checks coming in; but putting that into practice, writing your first sales letter, creating your first offer, that is taking the knowledge and turning it into reality. **So I would encourage you to move forward. Take the information you've read in this book already, and put it into play.** I would encourage you to take it from head knowledge to application immediately, because that is where you're really going to see breakthroughs happen—as you begin to actually do it.

Remember: as Gary Halbert said, **"You can learn more from movement than mediation."**

CHAPTER NINE

❖ ❖ ❖

There is *so much joy* that comes from the long-term effects of a life of <u>hard work</u>, <u>discipline</u>, <u>focus</u>, <u>goal setting</u>, <u>commitment</u>, and <u>daily striving to work towards your dream</u>.

The Joys of Hard Work

"There is so much joy that comes from the long-term effects of a life of hard work, discipline, focus, goal setting, commitment and daily striving to work towards your dream." That quote means a lot to me. For the most part, people are looking for a simple, boring 9-to-5 job. To me, entrepreneurialism is about is 5-to-9: getting up at five in the morning and working until nine at night. **It's all about discipline, and dedicating yourself to your business.** If you really enjoy what you do, then work is more of a hobby than actual work. You see people who spend hour after hour involved in all kinds of hobbies, because they're passionate about them; they enjoy them; they get absorbed by them.

That's the way work is to me, and to lot of other entrepreneurs I know. For example: this morning, I got up at four o'clock simply because I had an idea, and I knew that if I went back to sleep, I might forget it. **I had to get up to write this idea down.** It's for a project that I've committed to, a project I haven't really decided how I'm going to put together. I got this great idea, and so I had to get up to work on it—and the time passed quickly. **When I get lost in my work, it sometimes seems like hours turn into minutes.** You've experienced that before. In a sense, it's like being asleep; you may have been asleep for six or eight hours, but when you wake up, it seems that the time went by really quickly. That's the way it is when you're absorbed in work that you love.

There's a book that's sold millions of copies called "Do What You Love, and the Money Will Follow." I've got a little problem with that, because it's just too simplistic: some people just love to eat Mexican food or watch football, and if you do *only* those kinds of things, the money's probably *not* going to follow. **In my opinion, you need to find out what makes you the most money, and then fall in love with *those* things.** In this entrepreneurial world, the thing you need fall in love with most is marketing, which is simply all the things you do to attract and retain customers, and differentiate yourself from the competition. It's a great game. It's a great joy. There's so much to learn.

Recently, *Good Morning America* aired a clip about a 74-year-old female bodybuilder who's won some championships. She's only a few years older than my Mom, but she's a very attractive woman. Honestly, I don't usually think of 74-year-old women as being attractive; that's a little weird, and I mean it out of respect for her. She really looked good. She goes around the country working with other people in her age bracket, trying to get them to get off their butts and do something and move forward.

I love what she said: she talked about the three "Ds" that you need in order to succeed. The first "D" is **determination.** The second "D" is **dedication;** that's a great word to me, because commitment is related to dedication, and I love the whole concept of being committed. The third "D" is **discipline:** forcing yourself to do what you know is in your best interests, even if you don't feel like it. Now, here's the point: **When you're determined and dedicated, it makes discipline easy.** You have to put the first two in front of the third. And by the way, here's the key to determination: just get angry. Anger is the easiest emotion for most people, so just get angry about something. Most of us can turn it on pretty quick… or at least, I can. I tend to be a rebellious person, so I get angry easily. Anger can be converted into determination. Once you're determined, you make a decision that you're going to do something; then you become dedicated and committed to it, and the discipline follows.

Being an entrepreneur is really a way of life. As I've mentioned before, I think about it as like being a farmer; farmers don't punch time clocks. For every farmer I've ever met, it's a 24/7 thing. They have their seasons, but even in the downtime, in the winter when they can't be in the fields, they're still doing things like repairing equipment and getting ready for the season. It's a lifestyle, not just something that they just do.

That's what I'd like to try to encourage you to think about. **When it comes to business and making money, first of all see it as a game, see it as a hobby, see it as a *passion*.** The money's important, don't get me wrong; without it, you don't stay in business. But in my opinion, if you place it as your top priority, your decisions are almost always wrong. **So, get excited; get passionate about what you're doing. Be committed.** The more committed you are, the easier the work is. Again, think of a hobby, and realize that a business can be just like that. Think of all the hours that people spend on their hobbies, as many as they can, because it's something they're really interested in.

One of the things that comes to mind when I consider the quote I started this chapter with is the fact that **people value the things that they have to work for.** If things come too easily, they're not considered to be worth much. As a result, they're easily squandered or lost. On the other hand, the things you're committed to, the things you've worked hard for, are the things you place more value on. But there's a flip-side of the entrepreneurial spirit. Yes, you get to reap the rewards of your harvest, and that's a great thing; and you get to do some things that having a typical job wouldn't allow you to do. But if something goes wrong, it's your own damned fault! **If you didn't have the determination and the desire to stick to it, and work hard and build these systems, and do all these things I'm telling you here, then guess what? Your business is going to falter.** There's no pointing fingers here; in my case, if something goes wrong, I'm not about to point fingers at the people who work for me and say, "*You're* the reason that we're screwing up," or "*You're* the reason that things aren't getting done correctly." No. There's none of that. **The buck stops with me.**

And so, when it comes to those things like determination and the simple fact that it would be real easy to get up and go fishing some days, you have to tell yourself, "Okay, fine. Let's go fishing. But I know, and my wife knows, that there's a lot of work that needs to be done here… and who's going to do it?" I'll bet that's when you decide *not* to go fishing.

This quote I started this section with also brings to mind a whole host of different things, like the high school counselor who talked to me when I was a freshman in high school and told me, "You really need to study hard and try different things, and go into something that you truly enjoy. That way, it won't seem like such a grind." There's a lot of truth to that, and often they're speaking from experience—even if it's something that we, as freshmen, just don't want to hear. **Most people have no idea**

how difficult life can be. I remember sitting there and getting that speech. So does my friend and colleague Chris Hollinger, who wanted to be a stuntman or a movie star or an athlete—all those things that 14 or 15 year old boys wanted to be, without realizing they don't have a clue.

Chris tells me that when he was at school, especially before high school, he struggled at math. He suspects now that he really didn't apply himself. He didn't like it, and he was a little rebellious towards some of his teachers. But for whatever reason, he just didn't do well. But algebra—well, heck, that was something else. There was something about the way Chris's freshman year algebra teacher taught the subject that really helped him pick it up; and suddenly, he was good at algebra. He looked forward to going to algebra class every single day, and doing algebra homework, even though before then, for all those years in grade school and junior high, he'd dreaded math. But there was a spark there with that teacher; and ironically, she was just this tiny little woman, close to retirement. But when she taught algebra, is sparked with him, and every one of her classes just flew by. It was probably that class that carried him through his entire high school career and made him become a teacher later, because he looked at every class that he took afterward differently—all because of one good teacher who made algebra enjoyable.

True success really does boil down to finding that one thing that makes work seem like it's not work. There's probably been a time in your life where you found something that clicked with you, whatever that was, and time would just fly by... and the next thing you know it was midnight. Most of the time that I, and people like me, spend building systems and marketing and actually running campaigns… it's not like work. **It's a labor of love—but it does take that dedication, that discipline, and a desire to get it done that I mentioned earlier.**

One great example of this is Colonel Harland Sanders. Remember him? This guy ran a lot of businesses before he ever started Kentucky Fried Chicken, and he had a lot of great business ideas. He worked very hard his entire life. I've read a lot about him, and I've seen some stuff on cable TV about him; and I learned, to my surprise, that it wasn't until he was 65 years old that he hit it big with KFC. Even after KFC made it big, he worked until he couldn't work any longer. There are stories of KFC managers calling up their franchisees and saying, "The Colonel's here, and he wants to cook chicken." Well, you let the Colonel cook chicken, because that's what the Colonel wants to do! He was a big advocate of working hard for work's sake. **That's what that initial quote is all about: working hard for work's sake, because it's work that's worth doing.** *Always* apply your talents and energies in something that's worth doing.

Sam Walton is another great example. No one was thrown out of more K-Mart stores than Sam Walton; he took great pride in that. He also claimed that he'd been in more K-Mart stores than any other person, including the high executives of the company. Why was he in there? **He was spying!** K-Mart was his biggest competitor at the time, though that may be hard to imagine now. **He was totally dedicated, totally passionate, in it to win, in it with all of his heart—and that's the way entrepreneurs need to be.**

That relates very closely to the next chapter, so let's move on.

CHAPTER TEN

Great Marketers Are Hunters.

We are happiest when we're on the hunt. The bigger the hunt — the happier we are. *We must be reaching all the time.* All is well as long as our reach exceeds our grasp.

Great Marketers Are Hunters

Great marketers are hunters. **We're happiest when we're on the hunt—and the bigger the hunt, the happier we are.** We must be reaching all the time, and all is well as long as our reach exceeds our grasp.

For years, I saw all these rich people on TV talking about how money wasn't all that important to them. If you watch those interviews, you'll see the same thing repeated, over and over, by multi-millionaires and billionaires alike. That used to really upset me! How dare they say that; they wouldn't be saying it *at all* if they didn't have the money! I just wanted to throw whatever was in my hand at the TV; and I'd yell, "Okay, if it's not that important, give me some! I'll take it off your hands."

But now that we've achieved some success, I know the truth. **Money isn't of ultimate importance to the entrepreneur.** What's most important is just what we're talking about here: it's the hunt. **It's the chase. It's the reaching, always trying to exceed our grasp.** This is part of what drives entrepreneurs. True entrepreneurs must have huge goals; those goals help get them out of bed in the morning, and let them hit the ground running.

Here are a couple of top-of-the-mind examples from my own life. Remember how I mentioned getting out of bed at four this morning? That has to do with the new pet boutique I've mentioned. We're starting a retail store with the intention of eventually putting a thousand of our pet boutiques coast-to-coast. That's a very audacious goal, and yet we're very committed to it. We're very serious and passionate about it. It doesn't mean we're going to accomplish it; we have to make our first store work before we can do that. Now, by the time you read this, we'll have had our grand opening, which we've been planning all year. **It's been frustrating; it's been challenging; and it got me out of bed at 4:17 this morning—because I had an idea, and I knew if I went back to sleep, I'd forget it.**

A project like this is both challenging and stimulating at the same time. Sure, it's inevitable that we'll have problems implementing anything like this; **but in recent years, I've grown to believe that problems are actually a good thing.** I spent years running from problems, and I still can fall into that trap; so I don't want to pretend like I'm beyond it, because I'm not. But, for the most part, I see problems as wonderful things because they contain enormous amounts of energy. Admittedly, a lot of it is *negative* energy. **Nobody likes to deal with the pain of a problem; it's frustrating, yet you *can* re-channel that energy into good things.** It spurs you into action, and life is action; and business is accelerated life. The more problems you have, the more potential energy you have to get spurred into action and move forward as you should.

When you set out with huge goals, it's inevitable that you'll run into lots of obstacles along the way. Problems, challenges, frustration, confusion—none of these things feel good, but they spur you into action. You're motivated. **You want to achieve these goals; and by keeping your reach**

always beyond your grasp, you're always moving forward. That's where the joy is. That's what this Way is trying to say; the one before it, too. **All the joy in a business like this comes from moving forward, trying to achieve your goals, trying to make things happen.**

With our new wholesale printing club, we have a goal of acquiring one million members. Again, it's a huge goal. But there's an interesting quote by Daniel Burnham that goes, **"Make no little plans; they have no magic to stir men's blood."** I first read that quote about 25 years ago, and I recently encountered it again. Daniel Burnham, who lived 100 years ago, was a big thinker who did extraordinary things with his life. He had huge goals. And don't think for one minute that those entrepreneurs out there making big things happen are any different from you, by the way. They're no different whatsoever; **they just have huge goals, and they're committed to making those goals happen. It's like a game to them.**

The people around them don't often understand them, because they think these people are just greedy SOBs. They're thinking, *When is enough money going to be enough?* And I'm not saying that some entrepreneurs *aren't* just greedy SOBs, because I'm sure some are. **But one of the reasons why you see these people continuing to strive, reaching out and making new deals, is because they** *enjoy* **it.** It helps keep them alive. Maybe having huge amounts of money is part of their ego, **but the joy is really in building the business.** That's where they get their pleasure. That's what moves them forward. That's what gets them out of bed in the morning. **The money is all part of it, sure; it feels good.** But it's the joy of the work that really matters; it's the joy of building the business and setting goals and making it happen. That's the real driving force in their lives.

Again, it's the thrill of the hunt. It's not so much the success or potential failure as much as the energy that's generated in the business itself. **Some of it's about overcoming obstacles; some of it involves actually having to force yourself beyond your limitations,** or what you *perceive* as your limitations. **Some of it's learning how to do new things.** All that is necessary; you have to keep pushing, and that helps you feel alive. Business is life on steroids. **It's super-charged life, especially when your money is on the line, along with your credibility, your integrity and your business.** It's exciting!

Can you imagine a tiger on the prowl that isn't very, very focused? Being focused on your business is similar. It's that hunt that drives you; it's that exhilaration of doing and being and working with people from all over the country, and getting out there and getting in the game. My friend and colleague, Chris Hollinger, played basketball for a long time, and he compares business to athletics, to being ready to perform on the court or ball field—because athletics, especially basketball, is nothing more than unscripted drama in action. **Not everybody can get out there and perform; it takes practice and dedication.**

Chris played all the way through college, and once that part of his life was over, he needed an outlet for some of that competitive and intellectual energy and imagination. He says that back when he played, especially in college, they would have a drill where he would look at the other team and find reasons to get mad at them—whether it was how they looked, or the color of their uniforms, or whatever. He would even make up stuff —

for example, that they were trying to horn in on his girlfriend. It didn't matter what it was as long as he got mad, because **he knew that the emotion that would come out of it was good and useful, as long as it didn't overwhelm him.**

He says he did stupid things on the court sometimes, but it was the thrill of competing that mattered. Chris is one of five boys in his family—the one right in the middle—so he had to compete against the older ones and then he had to fend off the younger ones. For him, it's inbred; for me, it was something I had to work on a little. **But that competition, that thrill of the hunt, is what motivates real entrepreneurs to get up and get things done and to push themselves harder than they normally would. And the joy is never in the *catch*, by the way; it's in the *hunt*.** The irony is that people tend to stop trying once money is in the bank.

The first year that we were in the business, all this money just started coming in: hundreds of thousands of dollars. Before that, it was always a struggle just to keep a roof over my head. Some of the places I lived in were pretty bad; I was poverty-stricken for a number of years… and then, all of a sudden, hundreds of thousands of dollars were coming in, and I remember that I got so *depressed*. We were working with Russ von Hoelscher by then, and one day he called me up and said, "T.J., you haven't called me for a couple of months. What's going on?" I said, "I don't feel like talking to anybody. I'm just depressed." **In my mind, I had all these goals of making so much money, and when I did, I thought that it was going to somehow do something for me that it didn't.** It was still me looking back in the mirror every morning.

Russ helped straighten out my thinking a little. He said, "Look, you can only eat one good meal at a time. You can only sleep in one bed at a time. You can only drive one car at a time." Basically, I had to just enjoy what I had, one thing at a time, and not be depressed because I couldn't do it all at once. **Sure, the money is great; but what's even greater is this hunt, this chase—just setting the goals and reaching for more. That's where the real joy is.**

CHAPTER ELEVEN

Build "risk reversal" into every offer.

★ Risk Reversal is taking all the pressure away from the prospect or customer...

★ It's an irresistible guarantee.

★ It's a dramatic promise that they must gain a major benefit — or they not only get their money back — but they will also receive something of tremendous value!

This blows them away — and will get you a lot of attention and interest.

Build Risk Reversal Into Every Offer

This principal goes back to a specific marketing tactic: **risk reversal, which involves taking all the pressure away from the prospect or customer.** It's an irresistible guarantee; it's a dramatic promise that they *must* gain a major benefit, or they'll not only get their money back, they'll also receive something of tremendous value. **These types of offers get a lot of attention and interest, largely because they answer all the objections of the skeptics.**

Here's a good example. Recently, we produced our Dallas Seminar, an annual three-day seminar we typically hold in a large city—this time it was Dallas. It started on Friday and continued through Sunday. That event sold for $3,997, and we guaranteed everyone that they could stay up until lunch on Saturday, and if they were unhappy—if they didn't feel that the event was just right for them for whatever reason—all they had to do was go up to any of the staff members and say, "I'm not happy." That's all. If they did that, we'd instantly write them a check for all their money back. In fact, they could stay for the entire event, and if they *still* weren't happy after it was all over on late Sunday afternoon, they could get half their money back.

That's risk reversal. Basically, there was no risk whatsoever.

We realize that people are skeptical. We realize that there are a lot of offers other than ours that people can spend their money on. That's part of the rationale for risk reversal. **We're trying to do everything we can not only to take the pressure off our prospective buyers, but to stack all that pressure on our side of the table.** We understand the necessity of that. We're all a little bit fearful sometimes. We're afraid that people aren't going to come through on their obligations or promises, or that somehow, we're not going to be able to get our money back if we're not happy. **As a marketer, you need to answer that fear with a big, bold, audacious guarantee.**

When you use marketing principles like this one, you really set yourself apart from all the marketers who don't. And why *aren't* they doing this? A variety of reasons, I think. First, they're afraid that they're going to get cheated. If you have a risk reversal offer that's too lopsided, you can get taken to the cleaners. For instance, nine years ago, I did a "five times your money back" guarantee—that is, I had an offer where I promised that if you weren't happy, I'd give you five times your money back. Well, let's just say that I did it once, and I'll never do it again, because we had a lot of people who took advantage of that offer.

It was only a $5 offer for a discovery package, thank goodness; but many, many people gladly spent that $5 with the sole intention (I found out later) of getting $25 back. We sent out lots of checks for $25 before we decided that the project wasn't such a good idea for us, and didn't roll it out. **But while the project didn't work out, the spirit behind it was pure.** We've had lots of double your money back guarantees over the years, and they're effective— because it's just amazing how skeptical people are, and this helps you overcome your skepticism. **Just don't go overboard with it,** like I did with our "five times your money back" offer, because I guarantee, some people *will* take advantage of you!

Another reason that marketers don't do risk reversal is because they're afraid to… not because they fear getting cheated, but because they're selling inferior stuff they don't believe in and that doesn't represent real value. A third reason is because they're just not thinking boldly or audaciously enough. Either that, or they're so sold on what they're doing that they assume everybody else is going to be sold on it, too… and nothing could be further from the truth. **Just because you're absolutely in love with your product, service or opportunity doesn't mean that other people will be.**

You always have to assume the exact opposite, in fact; always, *always* **assume that the other person doesn't care one iota.** Remember Homer Simpson, that heavyset, lethargic cartoon character? Think of the average person who reads your sales letter as being like Homer—the most apathetic, laziest person you can imagine—and try to sell to that person. Go overboard. Make your case. Be bold with your offer. **If it's as good as you say it is, let your prospect know that you're backing it up with a guarantee that protects them in every way and gives them lots of good things.** Your response rate will improve dramatically.

Here's one last reason why people are afraid to make these bold, audacious offers: **they're afraid they're going to have to give a lot of refunds.** A lot of marketers don't want to give refunds; they want to take the money in and never send it back out. **But that's a terrible mistake!** About 13 years ago, I had the privilege of meeting the great marketer Brad Anton, who likes to say, **"If your refunds are too low, you're not selling hard enough!"** That was his whole mantra. In other words, yes, when you make an audacious risk-reversal offer where you say you're going to give people double or triple their money back, or you're going to let them keep all these free bonus gifts, or you're going to let them stay for half of the seminar and still get their money back—**well, you're going to have to expect that some *will* want their money back.**

But the increased number of sales you'll get because of your risk reversal promise will more than make up for the money that you pay back out. You will always make more money in the end by doing things like that. You have to be audacious and bold; because as Virgil, the ancient Roman playwright, once wrote, **"Fortune favors the bold."** That's absolutely true; fortune *does* favor the bold, and you can rarely be too bold or audacious in your marketing and advertising, no matter what the offer. On one hand, you're going to be building a case for why your product or service is worth a certain amount of dollars; on the other, risk reversal comes into play in a big way.

In many ways, it boils down to imagination. **Imagination can set you apart from all the other guarantees out there...** though admittedly, oftentimes I'll stick with a very plain vanilla guarantee, not going much beyond offering 100% of their money back if they're not happy. But it's good to use an imaginative method of risk reversal when you can, because it does help cut through the skepticism and all the other associated

---

problems. **Creative risk reversal helps build that offer's value in people's minds.** So arrange it so that if they want, they can get their money back or keep the set of Ginsu knives or that special apple peeler.

Being creative with your risk reversal will increase your sales; that's a great reason alone to do it. **But here's the big one: with risk reversal, you can really differentiate yourself from your competitors.** People will notice the difference between you and people who aren't imaginative with their risk reversal. This will work especially well if people know that if they don't like your offer, you'll step up to the plate and do exactly what you promised in terms of resulting that risk. **They're more likely to turn around and buy something else from you, because they know you're a person of your word.** The secret is simply to do what you said you would—and to go overboard to do that, if you must. I don't care what your market is, what your business is, this is an effective way to differentiate yourself from your competitors.

For example: this is one of those areas where good realtors can differentiate themselves from the bad ones. A good realtor has a guarantee in place, along with a good marketing system. You can go into any major metropolitan area in the country today, and you'll see the obvious differences between the good realtors, who have these guarantees, and those who do not. The good ones are generally those who guarantee they'll sell your house quickly, or they'll cut their commission—or you can fire them at any time. Some of them even offer to buy your house!

The reason they're confident with such a bold guarantee is because they've invested in their marketing

systems and their risk reversal promise. And sure, sometimes they *do* have to eat a deal. That's one of the things that nobody wants to do… which is why most marketers don't make these bold, audacious offers. They want everything to be one way, and that's their way. But that's a wrong-headed way to look at the business world. Back in the 16th century, Thomas Fuller said, **"Boldness in business is the first thing, second thing and the third thing."**

Again, fortune favors the bold.

CHAPTER TWELVE

Every prospect we seek is running around with a big sign around their neck that is flashing this message:

*"Please make me feel important!
And good about myself!"*

However, only those with trained eyes can see this sign.

Fulfill the strong desire people have to feel...

- Important
- Esteemed
- Admired
- Beloved
- Special
- Observed

And they will give you everything they have!

Make the Prospect Feel Important

This one may sound a bit manipulative, but it's vital, and I really don't think it's manipulative at all. The concept derives from the work of the great Dale Carnegie, who wrote *How to Win Friends and Influence People*. It wasn't his greatest book, in my opinion, but it sold millions of copies; it still sells like crazy today, and it's almost 80 years old. Here is the secret behind it, the quote that lies at the heart of this chapter: **"Every prospect that we seek is running around with a big sign around their neck that is flashing this message:** *Please make me feel important! And good about myself!"*

Only those with trained eyes can see this sign. Our job as marketers is not only to see the sign, but to fulfill the strong desire expressed by it. **It's up to us to make the prospect feel important, esteemed, admired, beloved, special and observed. When you do this, people will naturally gravitate towards you.** This *can* be manipulative, if you're doing it just because you want something back. But I feel that it has to go beyond all that. And again, I'm not going to take the high road here. I struggle with all this myself. I have my good days; I have my bad days. Maybe if I live to be a hundred, on my last, dying breath, I'll finally be there all the way; but I'm not there yet.

You have to make people feel important because they *are* important. That's the whole thing. They're important. They're sacred. When it comes to business, you should love your clients and customers—and not just because they're giving you money. **Learn to really care about your customers; try to feel their pain, try to connect with them.**

How to Win Friends and Influence People is just as relevant today as it was 80 years ago. If you don't want to take the time to read the whole thing (and you definitely should), just remember that one principle. **Always treat people as if they're important, because they *are* important.** It's easy to treat people well when they treat *you* well; that's the easiest thing in the world. It's when people aren't treating you so nice that's that it gets to be tough.

Now, I know some really good, top-notch salespeople who are absolute sharks. No offense to the industry in general, but a lot of these guys are used car salesmen. And I'll tell you what: when they're trying to sell you a car, they will wine you, dine you, tell you everything you want to hear—they're nice as can be to you. **But after you buy the car… well, they're not nice at all, especially when they're talking about you to other people.** Chris Lakey's brother is one of the true good-guy car salesmen, but having been around him, and having tried to sell cars himself, Chris says he's seen plenty of those sharks. They're wolves in sheep's clothing.

Marketing is a type of hunting; about going after the sale aggressively. This is not the same thing, folks. **Treating people as commodities is shallow and ultimately harmful, and that's often the culture that exists in a car lot.** That's not to say that all car lots have that culture, but many do. **Or consider the culture that existed at Enron,** where they were actually
120

manipulating and shortening the supply of energy so they could jack up the cost—and then joke about it.

Greed will reveal one's heart very quickly. And there's ample opportunity to take advantage of people, even though there's a lot of skepticism out there. **But if your goal is to build a strong business that isn't founded on taking advantage of people, you need to maintain a high level of honesty and integrity. At the same time, this quote tells us to believe in the fact that you do have to appeal to that human nature.**

Elsewhere, I've mentioned the need to enter into the conversation that's already going on in the hearts and the minds of the people you're selling to. The reason you want to do that is because your ultimate goal is not just to get their money right then, but to establish that person as a long-time customer. **You don't want a one-time sell; you want a relationship that builds on you doing what you say you're going to do, and taking care of your customers—while realizing that every single human being has their own particular and specific wants, needs, desires and problems.**

Now, some wants, needs and desires and problems are general to our species, and these are the realms that we can work in as marketers to help connect with them. Is this intended to help sell our products? Yes, of course. **But ultimately, the purpose is to help build a business.** So, when you talk about fulfilling these needs, you're tapping into basic human nature. **It helps to have that grounded in ethical behavior before, during, and after the sale.** It's not predicated on that ethical behavior; there are plenty of successful salespeople who *aren't* ethical. But they're not building the relationships that will truly

121

enrich them.

And yet the fact is, as a marketer, it's my job to ask people for their money. When I say something like, "I'm building a marketing system that extends my ability to sell on your behalf," what that really means is, "I'm not afraid to ask for the money." If you *are* afraid to ask, you're going to be a skinny salesman with skinny kids. **You can't worry about manipulating people. They want to you to make them feel special, so do that, and get beyond any reluctance to ask for the money.** They want you to offer them something that they can spend money on to feel good about themselves anyway.

Look, there's a lot that we can go into here about the psychology of a sale and the psychology of the people who make up your market, whether you're selling your plumbing service or making refrigerators. **Understanding human nature will help you capture more of your market share. Whenever you look at your specific market, you want to develop a very good, realistic picture of the people who comprise it.** What are their wants, needs, desires, frustrations and pains? How can you offer something that can help alleviate their pain and desires, help them get over their obstacles, their previous failures and frustrations? **That's what's important here.**

Look for things that are <u>HOT</u>!

"Whatever is current creates currency."

<u>STEP ONE</u>:

Find people to sell stuff to.

<u>STEP TWO</u>:

Find stuff to sell to those people!

123

Look for Marketplaces That Are HOT!

Here's a little quote that I love: **"Whatever is current creates currency." In other words, you have to strike when the iron is hot, in marketplaces where people are excited.** It's all about the marketplace; **the market comes first, *not* the product or service.** What you sell isn't nearly as important as who you sell to. A market, of course, is any group of people who have commonalities that cause them to buy whatever you sell. Years ago, we had something called the Money Machine Seminar, which was actually our very first expensive seminar — and we had this little quote hanging above the banner. Basically, it was this: "Step #1, find people to sell stuff to; Step #2, find stuff to sell to those people." **Look especially for niche markets, markets where people have something in common that they're rabidly emotional about.**

Our newest venture is a pet boutique. One of the reasons why we chose that particular business is because the market tends to be rabid; they're passionate about their pets. In fact, the huge ad that we created for our grand opening was headlined, "A New Store For Pet Lovers Only." So we're telling people that if you're *not* a pet lover, you're not going to feel at home in our store. But if you *are* a pet lover, you're going to walk into our store and you're going to say, "Man, this is totally cool!"

Just before we opened, a little girl walked in with her Dad.

3 STEPS TO INSTANT PROFITS!

Our staff was in there, setting things up; we were eight days away from opening, so we told them we weren't open yet, but to feel free to look around. And as they were walking around, the little girl goes, "This is the coolest thing that I have ever seen in my whole life." That's the response we're looking for! **It's an emotionally-charged thing.** In this case, it starts with the niche market: pet lovers, people who are passionate for their pets. Some of these people are freaks, and I'm one of them. I've got two dogs, and I'm always kissing on them and hugging them, and I spend a lot of money on them, and I worry about them constantly. Whenever I take them somewhere in the car, I leave the air conditioner running in the summer, or the heater running in the winter. I'm always looking for special things to do for them. **Most people who aren't pet lovers don't do things like that.** They feed their pets whatever dog food's on sale. They just have a whole different behavior, a whole different mindset.

It starts with the marketplace. You should look for niche markets. **Look for people who have something in common that causes them to buy things in an obsessive way.** Our parent company sells to opportunity seekers, the millions of people out there looking for ways to make money. **Opportunity seekers are a rabid marketplace; they're insatiable people who simply cannot get enough.** They buy all kinds of plans and programs, fill out all kinds of forms, join all kinds of mailing lists. And you might think, looking at these people from a rational perspective, "How many moneymaking programs can you possible own?"

In fact, when our head accountant started over two decades ago, during his first week of business he looked at what we were selling and told himself, "Jeez, I have to get my resume out there." **We weren't even two years old at that time, and he was thinking "Man, this company isn't going to make it."** And he *had* been around other small businesses that hadn't. **What he didn't realize was that we had tapped into a marketplace of millions and millions of people who are habitual, obsessive-compulsive purchasers of every single plan and program that they can possible afford... and even programs they *can't* afford.** Back then, people would write hot checks to us... heck, I used to do it myself. That's how we discovered this market. I used to be one of those people who bought all the plans and programs. I used to send hot checks to some of these companies... hoping that they would clear, of course, as I got the money in the bank on time. I never wanted to cheat anybody; but, hey, I was like a drug addict who had to have his fix. I was addicted to buying these programs. I **was a** *rabid* **buyer.**

It starts with the marketplace. **Look for groups of people who have some type of commonality that causes them to buy certain products and services, who look for specific benefits and advantages.** Once you find people to sell stuff to, find things to sell them, and then keep trying to find more things like that. People who are new to the business often wander around instead of focusing on a particular niche. They have this reoccurring worry, like a endless loop playing in the back of their heads: "What am I going to sell? What am I going to sell?" **Well, if you have a marketplace of people you've made an initial sale to, and if you're committed to serving those people, it's going to be easier than you might expect to develop products and services to sell to them.** After a while, you won't have the problem of wondering what to sell; the only problem is that there are *too many* ideas, and you can't possibly present them all. Then the problem becomes trying to decide which ones are a cut above the rest, and implementing them first. **By serving the customers, you'll be very focused on what those people want, and you'll gain an intuitive sense of what works and what doesn't.**

In the meantime, as you're just getting started, start collecting people's personal information. That's what we're doing with this new pet boutique. With all our correspondence, we're going to be constantly asking the customer to tell us what they want, what they can't find, what they like, and what they don't like. And we're going to reward them if they take the time to fill out the little forms we send them, with free points off their next purchase or special coupons... or *something* to constantly try to get behind their eyeballs, to get inside their heads, **so that after we're in that business a while, we'll have a good, intuitive sense of exactly what it is that they *do* want.**

While business can be complicated, especially when all the elements aren't working in your favor, **the basics are pretty simple.** When you're hitting on all cylinders and reaching the right market, and you're selling those people more of what you know that they want, and you've got a marketing system that drives it and helps you attract and retain the customers—well, then it's the easiest thing in the world. **Whenever it gets complicated, go back to this little two-step formula. It's all about attracting the right people, and then selling to them again and again. Offer related items that give them more of the same types of benefits and advantages they bought from**

you the first time.

This is one of the core principles of all business. Now, with this book, I'm digging deep and covering a lot of strategies. They're all useful, but this is one of the "must-knows" that you absolutely have to understand and internalize. **This one of those things you have to commit to memory. It needs to become a part of your business thought process—no matter what your marketplace is, no matter what you're selling, no matter if you're local or Internet-based.** This is a core strategy that you have to have down cold.

So look for things that are hot. **Find people to sell your stuff to, then find the stuff that you're going to sell to those people.** It really doesn't get any more complicated than that. **The problem is that most people reverse this.** They have an idea for a product or a service and *then* they ask themselves, "Okay, who would be interested in buying this?" They spend all their focus on figuring out what their product is going to be before determining who might buy… which is a mistake. For a retail establishment, a local store, that would look something like this: "I want to start a store. I'm going to sell these widgets here. Okay, now, I'm going to build my store. I've got my store all set up. You know, it took me a while to do that. Now that my store is open, I'm going to try to figure out who would be most likely to come into my store. I've got to find a way to make it work, because I need people to come into my store. So who are my people? Where are those people going to be found? Where can I advertise to reach those people? What kinds of things can I do in the advertising realm to get those people to know that I exist and that I have these widgets that I *think* that they would want?" And that's the way that goes.

The better approach, the *right* approach, is to identify the marketplace first—identify the who before the what. Who is most likely to be your customer? Who do you *want* to become the customer that buys from you over and over again? I know that seems a bit counterintuitive; most of us think, "Well, I don't know *who* until I know *what*. I have to know what I'm selling to know who's going to buy it." But that's not the right way to think about it. **Start with who you want to sell to.** Who do you want to become your very best customer? **Then find out what those people want.** That becomes the basis for your product or service line; not just what you sell them once or what you use as your core product, but all of the additional products and services and revenue streams that you create as you continue to do business with those people.

Let's take another look at the pet boutique we're opening. If you were able to be a fly on the wall and participate in all the conversations that happened between the very beginning of the concept and the reality of the store actually opening, you would probably have a lot of different feelings about the whole experience, and not all of them would be positive. In fact, many times throughout that process, you would probably think, "These guys are completely mad! They're crazy!"

The steps I just outlined to you, in my hypothetical example, are the way it usually works—where you first have a product or a service, and then you decide who your customers are going to be. **But we started out, months and months ago, by looking for a marketplace that was full of rabid buyers whom we knew were insatiable and would spend a lot of**

money trying to satisfy their desires. Instead of saying, "We want to start a retail store; what should our product be?" and then figuring out who to sell to, we started by saying, "Who could be a good customer, and what do those people want?" We looked at a lot of different marketplaces before selecting one.

We covered industries we knew had the potential to fill this need or meet our criteria. We looked at things like coffee, for example. Starbucks has raving fans who will spend a lot of money on coffee. If you have the right kind of coffee store, you can build a customer base from those people who really like coffee. Another marketplace we looked at was jewels and jewelry; people tend to spend a lot of money on those items, and there are some rabid buyers in that market. **In short, we looked at a lot of other possible scenarios before we landed on a pet boutique.**

We found, when we looked at the marketplace of people who bought pet food and pet items, that it was a crazy marketplace full of people who, well, sometimes seem like they don't think too much. Here's what I mean: in the end, a pet is just an animal. Some people barely even look at their pets, so the Wal-Mart special is all they buy for them. **But this is still a marketplace full of people who will spend thousands of dollars annually not only for medical treatment for their pets, but on things like fancy collars and leashes, and special water and food dishes and beds, and all kinds of accessories.**

They really do consider their pets a part of their family, and people would do anything for a family member. In many cases, they would do anything for their pets, too—so they want to feed them the best foods. If we can educate them on why premium-priced pet food is important, we can build a marketplace of people who don't mind spending a lot of money on food for their animals. **The long and short of it is, we started with the marketplace before we knew what we were going to sell, even before we knew exactly what shape our store would take… well before we knew it would be a pet boutique.**

We're focusing on pet owners who really do consider their pets an integral part of their family. They treat them like kids, they baby them and take them everywhere, and they buy them all kinds of things; they might spend several hundred dollars a month just buying toys and treats and goodies for their pets. The market as a whole apparently has plenty of disposable income, and they're willing to spend it. **That's how we came up with the pet boutique theme, but it all started with the broad marketplace that we wanted to serve. Then we narrowed it down to a niche in that marketplace that we felt had an insatiable appetite for certain kinds of products and services.**

So it starts with finding the people to sell the stuff to, and then finding out what you can sell to them. Our store will operate like this: now that we know who our marketplace is, we can get started. As people come in, we can refine what we offer based on their feedback. We'll change the products we carry, we'll make special offers to them, we'll do things to try to continue finding out what they want and continue to give them just what they want. A business isn't just a one-time sale; no, it's a constant, ongoing battle of trying to find what the customers want, and then finding the best, most profitable ways to give them those things. That applies to any marketplace you're in.

Identify the marketplace first. Start with the who and then add the what, and figure out what it is you're actually going to sell to those people.

You've hear the cliché that goes, "If everybody is your customer, nobody is your customer." It's a cliché for a reason. **It's not up to you to determine in advance exactly who that customer is.** For instance, in our retail store, our store manager has an idea of who she thinks the average customer is going to be. But Chris Lakey and I are standing back and saying, "Well, maybe you're right, maybe you're wrong. We don't know that yet." In almost every case, you run the ads that are designed to bring people to you, and *then* you slowly learn over a period of time what your customers have in common, so you can get a profile of who the average customer is. In this case, our manager thinks the average customer will be a young, stay-at-home mother. Chris and I are just watching, sort of amused, from the sidelines, because we know that that may be right, or that may be very wrong. We might find that our best customers are senior citizens.

You can never tell for sure who your best customers are going to be; that's why you do the marketing, and then watch things very closely.

CHAPTER FOURTEEN

Marketing is simply a 3-step process:

1. Attracting qualified leads.

2. Converting the highest percentage possible into first-time sales.

3. Re-selling the largest number of customers, as many times as you can, for the highest profit from each sale.

◆

These are the only 3 steps! However, each one must be done the right way.

Marketing Is A Three-Step Process

MARKETING IS SIMPLY A THREE-STEP PROCESS. **Step #1** is attracting qualified leads; **Step #2** is converting the highest possible percentage of those leads into first-time sales; and **Step #3** is reselling the largest number of those people as many times as you can for the highest profit from each sale.

Only those three steps matter, but each must be done the right way for all this to be effective, and they're pretty much tied together with the three ways to build a business, which I've outlined before. To review, the three ways to build a business are #1, to attract more customers who have never done business with you before; #2, to resell to more of those people more often; and #3, to resell those people more stuff every time you *do* sell them something. **It's all about generating leads, converting the highest percentage of those leads, and then developing relationships that cause people to come back and buy from you repeatedly.** All the money you want to make is in those relationships, assuming you have a large enough group of people to work with.

We're currently running ads to generate leads for our new pet boutique. They're pretty simple: we just have a notice of a grand opening, and there's a headline that basically says, "A New Store for Pet Lovers Only." That way, we're attracting the people we most want to attract. We don't want the people who are buying the cheapest dog food possible to come into the store just to check us out, knowing full well they're never going to become regular customers, because all our pet food is premium-based stuff that sells for two or three times more than the cheapest stuff in Wal-Mart. **It's all about attracting the most of the right kind of people that you possibly can.**

In this case, we're asking people in **Step #1 to come into our store.** In **Step #2, in an attempt to convert the largest percentage of people when they do come into the store,** we're trying to make them special offers—trying to do business with them initially. **Step #3 is the money step.** It's all about money, of course, but this is where the money really flows in. It's about doing business with those people for as long as possible and, of course, in a local environment, you're trying to get them to give you the names of their friends and family; **you're trying to turn them into little salespeople, rabid fans who not only come back and do more business with you, but bring their buddies along.**

As far as the relationship factor goes, you're trying to segment your customer base. You're keeping track of who buys the most stuff from you, of course, because those are your best customers. Or you can segment them by the type of items that they're buying. **Either way, you communicate with them on a regular basis.** Using the example of our pet boutique, we're going to host events fairly often: special sales, special educational events where we bring in speakers and the customers have to RSVP, things like that. **We'll be doing things to build relationships with our customers, so we can get to know them and they can get to know us.** That's how you develop trust, and figure out what it is that the market really, really wants.

One reason that I like this principle is that it's another formula; it keeps things simple. It's all about generating leads, closing the largest possible percentage of those leads, and then doing business with that percentage as much as you can. Somebody's not really a customer until they come back a few times; until then, they're just a prospect. **So think of this as a process, something that doesn't just materialize at once. It takes time to evolve, takes time to develop. So be sure to give yourself plenty of time. Be committed to the long-term success of your business.** Be willing to push on, through thick and thin.

This process applies to all businesses. We've been in the direct response business now for over two decades, where we meet face-to-face with very few of our customers—only a very small percentage at best. But it's *still* about these same three steps. We're doing all kinds of advertising and marketing to attract the largest number of the best qualified prospective buyers. **We usually use two-step marketing, where the <u>first step</u> is a low-cost or a no-cost transaction, which makes it easy for them to send away for something.** That's the first step of the marketing process. **The <u>second step</u> is where we try to convert the largest percentage of those initial leads to a one-time purchase of some kind that's related to whatever it was they responded to on the first step. And then we're staying in touch with them on a regular basis, trying to do as much business with them for as long as we possibly can.**

It all just sounds so simple—because it is. Now, it's not always easy to accomplish; in fact, it can be very difficult at times. But even when it gets the most difficult, just go back to the formula, back to the basics, and you can reconnect with the simplicity of it. **What will seem very confusing when things aren't working for you will be much *less* confusing when you go right back to this basic formula.** It doesn't get any more basic than this... and yet there are a lot of variations on the theme.

I want to encourage you, as you think about this strategy, to work backwards. A lot of times, when people are looking at how they want to attract customers, the first thing they do is think, "Well, okay, I need to bring in a lot of leads. I *know* I need leads. I can't build a business without generating leads first." **This is especially true as it relates to DRM, where you're trying to build a mailing list, which should be your ultimate goal.** Even in a retail establishment, you need to have a list of customer contact information, so you can communicate with them on a regular basis and do more business with them. So what you'll see happening is this: people will start by thinking that they need to build a mailing list, and that they need to generate leads. They've already identified a marketplace; this is assuming that you've done their preliminary work. You've started with a marketplace, so if you know that you've developed a product that your marketplace wants really badly, you've done a good job there. **Now you need to attract as many of those people from that marketplace as possible, to get them to respond so you can follow this formula.**

But if you're not careful, you'll do too good a job of attracting leads—and you won't do a good enough job of qualifying them. Sure, you've built a nice list of people who have raised their hands and requested information from you... but if you haven't been selective in how you've done it, that list will turn into a nightmare to manage. **If all you have are tire-**

kickers who raised their hands because your product was cheap or free, you'll have a list that you can't do much business with. It's not profitable, because you haven't done a good enough job of qualifying the people on that list… **and you end up with a mailing list that's pretty much useless.**

I find it interesting to hear people talk about how hard a time they have generating leads — because if you've studied sales copy, if you've become a good copywriter and you know how to create offers that sell, then you should have no problem getting people in your marketplace to at least raise their hand and request free information from you. **So *getting* leads shouldn't be a problem if you've done your homework well and have become a good student of DRM.** But you *can* have too many leads coming in, and if you're not able to convert those leads, they're useless.

Start with the end in mind, and remember that your ultimate goal is not *just* to build a big mailing list, it's to build one that you can mail to profitably over and over again. As you'll notice in Steps #2 and #3, you need to convert the highest percentage possible into first-time sales, and then resell the largest number of those people as many times as you can for the biggest possible profits. The way you do that is by focusing not so much on raw numbers or the sheer quantity of leads that you can bring in, but on the quality of those leads. **It's not the size of the mailing list that's important; it's the quality of the mailing list.**

We have a good friend in Dallas who has made millions on a list of fewer than 300 people. It's probably larger than that now, of course, but it wasn't a few years back. I always think of him when I think of this reality, because so many people think, "Oh I've got to have a list of thousands and thousands of people," or, "My list isn't as big as yours; I can't do what you've done." Wrong! **Those kinds of excuses just wash away under the reality that it *doesn't* take huge numbers. It just takes a good list. It takes a list that's grown the right way, and it doesn't matter how big it happens to be.** If you've done a good job of qualifying the people on your list, they can become good, lifelong customers worth a substantial amount of money to you and your business. So qualifying your leads is very important. **Don't worry about having too small a list; worry about having too big a list that's not qualified.**

Attracting the qualified leads is Step #1, yes, but you start with the end goal in mind. **Remember that you want to attract as many qualified leads as possible, because the goal is to sell to your customers and sell to the people on your list, over and over again.** One sale does not a customer make. Yes, you got somebody to come into your store or to your website to buy something, but it's the subsequent sales that solidifies that relationship. Yes, you need that first-time sale; but don't think that just because someone bought from you once, that they're going to turn into a good customer.

There's a story about a dry-cleaner who understood a little about what it took to be a success. He ran an ad that said, basically, "Bring us a trash bag full of your dry-cleaning and we'll clean it absolutely free." That was a one-time free offer, so he had a lot of people take him up on it. Then he sent an offer just to the people who took him up on that offer and said, "Well I can't do free dry-cleaning for you forever... but if you bring another bag in, I can do it for half price." He did something like that one more time with just the people who responded to the second offer. **Ultimately, he found that if he could get someone into the store for just three visits, they were never going to take their dry-cleaning anywhere else unless he screwed up really badly. Otherwise, they would be a customer for life.**

You've got to do something like this guy did, to **identify the people who are going to be your best customers.** They'll come from your broader list of leads, including those who buy from you once; but these are the people who have proven to you that they've valuable, because they buy again and again. **It's like a big funnel: you have a giant list of qualified leads that becomes a smaller list of one-time customers that gets trimmed down to an even smaller list of repeat customers, and** *those* **are the ones you need to spend most of your time and energy on.** Your goals should be to resell to your existing customers over and over again for the highest profit margin possible from each sale. **It's easier, and therefore can become cheaper, to sell to people who already know you, like you, and trust you.** That smaller list of people becomes easier to communicate with.

Those are the kinds of people you can send an email to and invite to come into your store for a sale, and you know they'll respond. **You make them a good offer that they can't refuse, and you communicate with them in a way that they're agreeable to.** If you've never emailed your customers before, don't think that you can just send them an email and have them all respond. Some of them may, but if you always communicate by direct mail, then continue doing that. If you always communicate by email and you know that your customers respond that way, then fine, you can continue doing that. **The main thing is that once you've got that relationship established, it's more cost-effective and more profitable to continue doing business with them.**

As you're doing this, you're continuing to generate new, qualified leads so that you can turn some of them into sales and then, eventually, get some on your preferred customer list. **You repeat this process as part of an overall system or strategy of list building, even as you continue serving your existing customers.** When all this is working like it's supposed to, **it can become a well-oiled machine that just sucks in the profits automatically.** Hence, the name of our old Money Machine Seminar; because when you get all those elements right, it really *does* work like a well-oiled machine. **When people keep coming back, it makes it easier for them keep coming back. People are creatures of comfort and habit.** If they feel comfortable with you, they're unlikely to seek out some other business; **they'd much rather do business with somebody they've already given their business to before, assuming they've been happy with the results.** With all the complexities in today's busy world, it's always great to deal with people who know you.

My wife drinks a couple of glasses of wine at night. Every time I go into the store to buy her wine, they just know what I want. I just stand at the counter and they go get it for me; I don't even have to say a word. **It's nice when you have people that you've done business with often enough that it's a shortcut to deal with them.**

CHAPTER FIFTEEN

The best ideas come to you in the heat of the moment!

Write down your best ideas when they are new — and when you are first getting started and very excited!

- <u>These ideas are HOT</u>! You'll need them later on when you are cold!!!

- Ideas are like slippery fish! Hard to hold onto! So you must capture them fast!

The Best Ideas Come To You In The Heat Of The Moment!

You've got to write down your best ideas when they're brand new, when you first get excited about them. These ideas are hot, and you need them later, when your mind is cold. **Ideas are like slippery fish; they're hard to hold onto, and you've got to capture them fast.** You also have to capture their enthusiasm.

Right now, we're busy getting our pet boutique off the ground. We ultimately plan to get other people into the business and, as far out as it may sound, we're already working on the sales material to sell the business opportunity; so we're busy, right now, working on the original sales copy that will ultimately be edited, rewritten, fine-tuned, filtered, and finalized. **Why are we starting on it now? Because *now* is when it's exciting to us.** You've got to strike while the iron is hot, which is why we're doing it while the whole business is still pretty much in a fantasy mode, because we haven't run into any big problems yet. **It's all just excitement, excitement, excitement.** That's the magical period when the purest ideas, the best ideas, tend to appear.

In the real world, there's no perfect business; there's always going to be an uphill climb. **There will be problems to be surmounted, obstacles to overcome; and this can just eat up your enthusiasm.** I see this quite often, especially in the information marketing business. **When people get excited**

about an information product, they'll often go ahead and develop it based on their enthusiasm; sometimes it will take them months, even years. By the time they get it done, when they go to writing the sales material, the thrill is gone. The magic, enthusiasm, the excitement, the passion, the desire, the zeal, the energy has evaporated, so the sales copy they write is flat and boring. Maybe the product really *is* outstanding, but the sales material designed to sell it is dull and tired, so the product flops. **That's why one of the core secrets of effective copywriting is to strike while the iron is hot.**

Ideas lead to more ideas. If you want to get some really good ideas, you have to come up with a *lot* of ideas. Sometimes your first ideas are good, and sometimes they suck. **The secret of brainstorming is to generate the largest number of ideas and to do it while you're excited.** Also, this is a creative thing. I've discussed creativity before: we all start out being creative, before it's washed out of us. Little kids are tremendously creative. They have make-believe friends and can entertain themselves for hours. They've got great imaginations and they like stories. They like to be read to. They like to draw and paint.

But as we get older, we tend to get sort of locked in. It's possible to retain that creativity, if you're encouraged to by certain adults and teachers; the rest of us, however, have to rediscover it within ourselves. **Because, you see, we don't actually *lose* it; we just become more tradition-bound as we age.** The creativity is there, but it may be rusty, like an old knife. Well, you can scrape off all the rust and resharpen that knife to reclaim a fine, sharp cutting edge. **And it *does* take work to be creative. The most creative people are the ones putting the**

most into it; don't be fooled into thinking otherwise. Maybe some people *do* have more of a talent for creativity, but that shouldn't stop you. **You've got to work at it.**

One of the ways I keep my creativity sharp is to get up early and get to work writing and working on my ideas. I've mentioned this a number of times before. One recent morning, I woke up between projects, in the sense that I didn't have any deadlines really pushing at me. I did have other writing projects, but they weren't deadline-bound; nevertheless, I forced myself to work on one project. For the first 20 minutes, my progress was very slow; working that project was a real struggle. But once I got beyond that, the creativity kicked in and I really started getting into the flow of it. Pretty soon, I had six single-spaced pages of 14-point type. I probably wrote close to 4,000 words by the time I was done.

The point I want to make here is you don't always start out enthusiastic—but if you just stay with it, you can get into it. It's just like exercising: the first 10 minutes might be hell, but from minute number 11 on to whenever you stop, you get into it and it becomes easier. You have to force yourself to do it in the beginning, sure, but soon you're going with the flow. **So pick a time of day and release your creativity.** For some people, like me, it's early morning; for some, it's late at night; and for others, I suppose, the best time is in the afternoon…

But work at it as much as necessary, and find somebody else to work with if you can. I work with Chris Lakey this way, and we feed each other ideas and connections that one or the other of us might never have come up with, and we'll go back and forth in developing our concepts to their maximum expression. **This results in a kind of magical synergy of two people who share one common goal, who are moving forward in the same direction, who can work together, brainstorm together.** All it takes is one more person to make the difference… though of course you can brainstorm with yourself, in the sense that you can think on paper. Your hand is connected to your brain, so when you write you connect with higher parts of yourself, a more creative side of who you are. But you should brainstorm with other people as much as you can, too.

Last but not least, in order to come up with the best ideas, you have to set some pretty big goals. **You've got to have something huge that drives you.** Some of the entrepreneurs out there are just amazingly driven; you've probably seen some of them in action. People will shake their heads and say, "Man, that guy's special! He must be incredibly talented!" Well, maybe that person *is* different, **but what's behind that difference—which you often don't see—is that they're driven by big goals, dreams, and desires.** That's what's missing if you're not as driven as you need to be. **It starts with the goals, the desires, the concepts.** If you take them seriously, you become dedicated to achieving those goals, and you'll get better ideas as you go along.

I think one of the worst things you can do is *not* have a way to capture all your ideas. For example: this has often happened to me, and I hear other people talk about this, too. **You wake up in the morning, and you remember that you had an idea overnight. Well, when this happens to me, if I don't write that idea down in the middle of the night, I lose it.** I might wake up in the morning knowing I'd thought of something when I was up in the middle of the night… but I can't remember what it was. Sometimes I can grasp what it was about in general, but I'll never remember the specifics. For some people, this might boil down to what they were planning to have for dinner, or the fact that they need something from the grocery store. For me, and people like me, it's often something more important. I've already told you about the morning when I forced myself to get up and go to work earlier than normal because I had ideas rattling around in my head... **because if I hadn't gotten them down on paper, they would have been gone by the time I woke up.**

You have to have a way to capture those ideas. **Chris Lakey has an iPhone, and he uses the audio recorder feature to capture his ideas. It also has a notepad function, so he can jot down a note if he prefers to write it.** If he writes a note, it automatically sends him an email that reminds him what his note was about, so he doesn't even have to remember that he needs to read his note!

The human brain is a pretty powerful thing, and it's interesting to realize the number of ideas and thoughts that pass through your mind on a daily basis. **It's astounding, because you're thinking about things *constantly*.** As I'm writing this, I'm thinking about what I'm going to say next, and all these ideas are going through my brain at a nonverbal level, even as I'm typing, rattling through possible scenarios. Your brain is always working, even if, in most cases, it's working on trivial things like whether you should have steak tonight or macaroni and cheese. Some decisions are important; some are not. **But there's always plenty going on in your brain, and it's the ultimate tool for marketing—*if* you use it in the right way.**

3 STEPS TO INSTANT PROFITS!

Ideas are going to hit you at the oddest times. You can't really take your phone in the shower with you, or a notepad for that matter; but you should still have one handy nearby, in case ideas hit you at those moments. You can always hop out of the shower and write an idea down. You never know when they're going to strike, and what happens is that you tend to remember the ones you focused on for some other reason. Let's say the idea came into your brain and for whatever reason it stuck, and it became one of the few ideas you ran with, and maybe eventually you got around to writing it down. But that doesn't happen that often. Usually, all you remember is that there was something you were supposed to remember, but you can't recall what it was, and you end up regretting that you didn't write it down.

Admittedly, not all your ideas will be good. Some will be, and others will turn out to be average, while many more prove to be duds—useless for anything important. **But you can never be sure, from the outset, which category they're going to fall into. The best thing you can do is capture all your ideas. Get** *everything* **down.**

The point of this particular strategy is that the best ideas come to you in the heat of the moment... and you never know when that "heat" is going to come. Sometimes it's in the eleventh hour, when a project deadline is bearing down on you. Sometimes it's when a project is in an infant stage. One of the things that Chris and I like to do when we have an idea is to take a moment to write a few paragraphs about that idea immediately, while it's fresh and new. **If it's a good one, or something we think might be workable, we'll spend some time jotting down some notes right there.**

Now, it's one thing to just write down the core idea; it's another thing to put several paragraphs of sales copy together. **What we find is that by spending a little time to gather our thoughts on paper, to follow through with an idea, we may be able to grow that idea into something profitable.** So once you've had the thought, take it beyond that infant stage. Think it through a little more. **Continue writing and let it grow and expand, and see if it's not something bigger than what you originally thought it was.** Maybe you'll struggle a little along the way; maybe all you'll do is write a few sentences, and it won't get very far. **The important thing is to get it down while the idea is fresh; that's when you're actively thinking about it.** Even if it comes to not much, put it down and revisit it later to see if it doesn't stimulate some new ideas.

And be sure to write down as much as you can. I've had times in the past where I've jotted down a note, and when I go back and look at it later, I have no clue what I was trying to say. The thought wasn't coherent. As I look back on it, I'm not sure what I was trying to convey or even what I was trying to remember. **Writing down a paragraph or two about it will help you remember what you were thinking about later.** So if you've got an idea for something, carry that idea through; and when you go back to review it later, you'll have a reference point and more information to go by.

Often, when ideas first come to you, or when you're working on a project and you're thinking things through specifically for that project, those ideas become the foundation for all your future thinking. Let's say you're serving a specific marketplace, and you've got an idea for a new product. It's a baby idea; you've written some notes on it, no more. As you start to expand on those notes, things will sometimes evolve around that initial central thought. Think of it as a solar system: you've got the sun, and you've got a bunch of planets circling around the sun, but the sun is the central focus that everything else orbits. **Your first ideas are like that sun.** All of the other ideas that come afterward will flow from that central thought, so it's important that that core idea gets some TLC, and gets the "watering" it needs to develop, because all of your other ideas will sprout from that basic concept. **You may change things, you may adapt things, but typically you head down a road leading from that original idea.** The journey from the concept to the actual implementation of that idea flows outward from that original thought process. **It's important to get everything down, get it all on paper, and then spend some time working on that idea and letting it grow.**

I like the concept that ideas are like a slippery fish. They're hard to hold on to so, you must capture them fast. If you don't capture them, if you don't get clarity on those ideas as soon as possible after you have them, before you know it, they'll be gone for good. There might be an abstract thought trace remaining about the idea, but the actual idea you had will be gone, and you probably won't get it back.

So capture those ideas when they're hot. In the heat of the moment, write down a few paragraphs. Write down other, associated ideas stemming from that, so you have a reference point when you go back—and not just once sentence or one idea that's easily forgettable, or you might not remember what that idea was all about!

CHAPTER SIXTEEN

❧Cold Calling Sucks!☙

Build a marketing system that automatically brings you qualified prospects that have expressed a great interest and are very likely to buy.

It is <u>not</u> the job of your sales rep to cold-call and develop their own prospects.

Cold Calling Sucks!

The statement above might be a tad controversial, but it's stone cold true. Cold calling is where you call people whom you *think* might have an interest in whatever it is that you're selling, and you make them a sales pitch. **Well, it's hard to build a business based on cold calling. Instead, you should build a marketing system that automatically brings you qualified prospects who have expressed a great interest in what you're selling, and who are very likely to buy.**

You know, when I started out in sales, the company I worked for expected me to develop my own leads—and that's the way a lot of companies do things to this day. They want the salesperson to make it happen, to go out there and drum up the business… and they know that most *won't*. Here's an example of how that works: a lot of direct sales companies will hire a hundred sales people. They know that their salespeople are going to go work in their warm markets—friends, family, co-workers, neighbors, associates, people that they've known all their lives, etc. That's going to bring the company a little revenue.

Once most of the salespeople have worked their warm markets, though, that's going to be enough for them. They're not going to go any farther. So, the companies look for people with huge families, or who are plugged into a big church or heavily involved in the community at some level. Once they train those people, they kick them out to go work their warm market and generate some revenue for the company. **Maybe one or two out of a hundred make it long-term, and they just keep that machine going; the company keeps hiring people and dumping them out and let them work their warm market.** They would love if those people started cold-calling people, and they hope they will, and that's the only way for a salesperson to really make money in that kind of situation... but they don't really expect anyone to do it, beyond the tiny percentage I've already mentioned.

I think that the days of cold calling should be over, because DRM is such a powerful way for companies to develop leads for their salespeople to work. **It's expensive, but you end up with so many more warm leads to sell to.** In my opinion, **it's the *company's* job to bring in the highly qualified leads**—people who've raised their hands and said, "Yes, I'm interested!" Those people have expressed a desire for the types of products and services the company is selling; they've bitten on an offer that was made to them, which leads you to believe that they're great potential prospective buyers who really *do* have a lot of chance of quickly buying whatever it is you're selling.

Now, in the next secret, we're going to talk specifically about two-step marketing. For right now, though, **I just want to say that when you start thinking about lead generation, two-step marketing is the fastest, safest, cheapest, easiest way to do your marketing.** Think about a dating ad. Even if you've been happily married forever, spend some time looking at some of those ads if you're interested in two-step marketing and the essence of what it is—and you'll see that they're trying to attract a specific person. The person who is looking is talking about things that they themselves are interested in: country music, line dancing, fishing, sports, and the like. They're looking for somebody who has an interest in the things they like; or at least they want to manage the reader's expectations and let them know that, hey, here's who I'm, here's what I'm interested in. Otherwise, they tell you what they're *not* looking for. *If you're a cigarette smoker, don't apply. No drugs, no drinking, no drama.* I've seen the funniest things in some of these dating ads; they really are amusing to read.

The authors of these ads are trying to attract a specific type of person, as well as trying to repel everyone else. **That's exactly the mentality you need when you're doing lead generation.** If you open the funnel too wide and aren't specific enough about what you're looking for and what you're *not* looking for, you're going to bring in a bunch of people who aren't well qualified—whether you're looking for a mate, or for prospective buyers for the products and services you sell. **If you're too narrow, too specific, if you go into a lot of details, then you're going to generate fewer leads—but they're going to be more highly qualified, so there's a process of testing involved here.**

And also, we're talking building a good marketing system that works like a well-oiled machine. **It generates leads automatically, and then those leads are closed through a series of follow-up messages, or by the salespeople themselves.** That's about how easy business is. Now, there are some exceptions; but as a general case, most businesses are all about generating leads—that is, getting people to take a specific action, which might be coming into your store, calling you up for a free bid, sending for a free booklet or DVD, whatever. **The idea is to get a prospective buyer to take certain steps that you want them to take, which proves to you that they really are serious; and then it's just about closing those sales.**

You do that by making people a specific offer designed to convert those leads into first-time buyers, and then it's all about trying to get them to come back repeatedly to do more business with you. At M.O.R.E., Inc., DRM is our chosen avenue for that. Even when you do have a customer base, you're still generating leads; you're still running special promotions, trying to get a percentage of those people on your customer list to come back and bite on another offer. That's because you've got to stay in touch with your customers. **Research on why people don't come back and do more business with the companies they've done business before reveals that the number one reason was because the company failed to remain in contact with them... not because of price or poor service.** The customer just forgot about the company. People are busy, so you have to stay in touch with them, keep reminding them you exist, keep offering them great deals.

That's still part of your marketing system, because **all the profits you want to make within your business comes from the repeat business.** You still have to find a way to get them to come back again and again. You can't just expect your salespeople to do all the work for you. **You've got to do things to get people to take that first step, and *then* let your salespeople follow up and work on those leads and close them.**

Now, we'll have more to say about this in the next secret;

but the fact is, **before you can build a marketing system to generate leads, you first have to know the perfect prospective buyer you're looking for.** What is it that they really want? How do you reach those people? And how do you cut through all the clutter, all the fog, in between you and them? **Simple enough: you have to develop special offers aimed specifically at them.** You have to realize just how much apathy that there is in the marketplace. The bottom line is people really don't care about you and your company; they're too overwhelmed with their own lives to care. They're inundated with all their own responsibilities, obligations, headaches and hassles. They aren't really thinking about you; **so to *get* them thinking about you, you've got to do things that are bold and outrageous—things that get people to take action.** Right or wrong, good or bad, in this overcrowded, over-competitive marketplace where there are so many available choices and options, you really *have* to do things to stand out. You may have to go over the top in ways that you might not necessarily want to.

Chris Lakey once spent about a year trying to sell cars. Now, there are a couple of ways you generate leads for selling cars, other than just talking to people that you know. That's the old standby: there are probably at least a few people in your family who are ready to buy cars, and the idea is that if they know you sell cars, they'll come buy them from you. But with prospects who don't know you, there are two things that happen. One is called the "up system," and that means that when someone comes on a lot and it's your turn to be up, you go and work with that prospect. So, you try to be up as many times as you can throughout the day.

3 STEPS TO INSTANT PROFITS!

At the dealership Chris worked for, there was a system for being up. **After you had a turn, you went to the back of the line and worked your way back up the list; and when you were up again, you took the next customer on the lot.** You just went around and around that way, and tried to talk to as many people as possible. Sometimes you'd get a customer who would be on and off the lot really quickly, so you would get back in the queue real fast; other times you'd get someone who wanted to test drive several different cars, and you'd talk to him for a few hours... and sometimes the deal would happen, and sometimes it wouldn't. And then you got back in line. So, some days you talked to a few people, and some days you talked to a bunch.

The other way was to do cold calling, which could literally involve picking up the phone book and just randomly calling people, saying, "Hey, how old is your car? Have you thought about trading it in? We're looking for some good cars." Or you could talk to people on the street, or in a bar, and say, "Hey, I noticed you just got out of such-and-such a car. We happen to be looking for that kind of car to add to our pre-owned inventory." Or you might say, "I know a buyer who might be interested in that car. Have you thought about trading it in? It's a good time to trade."

When you work your cold prospects, you drum up business any way you can. Like I said earlier, though, cold calling—all cold prospecting—just sucks. It's a tedious, slow process. **You end up annoying people, because they don't like to be cold-called (whether face-to-face or literally on the phone).** It's a bad way to do business, and there are smarter and more efficient ways to do it. That's where this leads to: **building a marketing**

system that automatically brings you qualified prospects who have expressed an interest in what you have, and who are likely to buy what you have to offer. As this relates to the car business, Chris tells me that he remembers seeing and hearing about people who were really good salespeople, because they'd put together marketing systems of some kind and were bringing leads directly to them. They weren't having to cold call.

Back when Chris was selling cars, he was just there trying to earn a paycheck; he wasn't really interested in marketing. But he did see people doing that. And I've heard of people in the real estate business who did the same thing. Rather than accepting the traditional way of selling in real estate, where you're just working prospects and trying to build relationships with people and then hoping they'll remember you when they're ready to sell their houses, **these people developed systems for attracting people in the market.** They would run ads, for example, that offered a free report to demonstrate how to get the most out of your home when you sold it; and, of course, anybody who responded was probably trying to sell their home, which meant that you could work that person and try to get them to come aboard as your client.

The main thing here is that you want to create a system that does all that work for you, as opposed to cold calling, where you're just trying to call as many people as possible and get somebody to say yes, or to at least take the time to listen to your offer. This is a system for attracting leads. You don't chase after them; they chase after you, which makes selling to them easier in the long run.

Here's an interesting side note. Recently, Chris had a

3 STEPS TO INSTANT PROFITS!

salesperson come to his door selling security systems; **it was the second time Chris had had a door-to-door salesman come by within a few weeks.** I've already discussed the fellow selling the household cleaning solution. This time, the person was trying to sell a form of insurance, and it was interesting to listen to him give his presentation. In a sense, people like that are doing the same thing face-to-face that you would cold calling somebody. They don't know that you're interested; maybe you already have a security system, or maybe you've thought about a security system and don't want one... maybe you do. Door-to-door salesmen don't know you from Adam. They just go and knock on doors, hoping that somewhere they can drum up some business. At the time, it was quite hot—and I can't imagine wanting to go door-to-door, sweating the whole time as I walked around the neighborhood. **Frankly, that's not really a smart way to attract qualified prospects.**

There's a much better way. You need to identify a marketplace, and how you should focus on *that* before you worry about the product. You start with a marketplace and find out what people in that market want the most, then you set out to develop products and services that give them exactly that. **A good marketing system plugs into that existing market, bringing you qualified leads: people you actually know are interested in what you have to offer.** It's one thing to have an offer that you know that people in your marketplace *may* want, and another thing to have an offer that people have demonstrated interest in.

Oh, you *could* just sell the product without trying to develop leads first. Let's say you had a product that sold for

$500, and you wrote an offer and made it available to the people in your marketplace. You would hopefully have a certain number of people who would send you $500 for your product… but starting out, you couldn't guarantee that. **This is called a direct one-step marketing approach. All you're trying to do is get people to buy your product out of the blue, without developing leads first.** Well, a better method is to first attract a group of people who have expressed some interest in your offer. That's called two-step marketing.

Basically, you're building a list of people who *are* interested in what you're selling; and then, from that list of prospects, you develop promotions to get them to buy your products. In this case, it would ultimately be a $500 product, and you would start by getting leads who requested information of some kind from you, who took some initial action. **All those leads would then become a part of a list that you promoted your main offer to. You might have a hundred people who raised their hand and requested information, and in so doing, they became your prospects.** They've proved their interest by sending for whatever you offered: a report, or an audio program, or something else they requested from you for free or at low cost. Of those hundred people, a smaller number, let's say five or ten, became customers by actually buying your $500 product. **You see, your goal is to sell the main product, but first you have to build a list of people who are interested in what you have to offer.**

www.ingramcontent.com/pod-product-compliance
Lightning Source LLC
Chambersburg PA
CBHW020206200326
41521CB00005BA/256

* 9 7 8 1 9 3 3 3 5 6 8 4 6 *